Northern COMFORT

New England's Early Quilts

1 7 8 0 - 1 8 5 0

Northern COMFORT

New England's Early Quilts

1780-1850

From the collection of Old Sturbridge Village

Lynne Z. Bassett and Jack Larkin

Photographs by Thomas Neill

Rutledge Hill Press®

Nashville, Tennessee

Published by Rutledge Hill Press®, 211 Seventh Avenue North, Nashville, Tennessee 37219.
Distributed in Canada by H. B. Fenn & Company, Ltd., 34 Nixon Road, Bolton, Ontario L7E 1W2.
Distributed in Australia by The Five Mile Press Pty. Ltd., 22 Summit Road, Noble Park, Victoria 3174.
Distributed in New Zealand by Tandem Press, 2 Rugby Road, Birkenhead, Auckland 10.
Distributed in the United Kingdom by Verulam Publishing, Ltd., 152a Park Street Lane, Park Street, St. Albans, Hertfordshire AL2 2AU.

Cover, page design, and typesetting by Harriette Bateman

Library of Congress Cataloging-in-Publication Data

Bassett, Lynne Z., 1961–
    Northern comfort : New England's early quilts, 1780-1850 : from the collection at Old Sturbridge Village / Lynne Z. Bassett and Jack Larkin : photographs by Thomas Neill.
        p.   cm.
        Includes bibliographical references and index.
        ISBN 1-55853-655-8

        1. Quilts—New England—History—18th century—Themes, motives.   2. Quilts—New England—History—19th century—Themes, motives.   3. Quiltmakers—New England—Themes, motives. 4. Quilts—Massachusetts—Sturbridge—Themes, motives.   5. Old Sturbridge Village. I. Larkin, Jack, 1943–   .   II. Neill, Thomas, 1950–   .   III. Old Sturbridge Village.   IV. Title.

NK9112.B39   1998
746.46'0973'09033—dc21   98-5678
                                                                                                          CIP

Printed in the United States of America
1 2 3 4 5 6 7 8 9—00 99 98

Contents

Foreword

Set in the rolling hills of central Massachusetts, Old Sturbridge Village is an outdoor museum of early American history. Nearly forty carefully restored historic structures from all parts of New England along with a landscape of fields, fences, gardens, roads, and woodlands set the stage for this re-created 1830s community. Historically costumed staff share the work, family, and community life of early nineteenth-century rural New England with hundreds of thousands of visitors each year. Through its collections, research, exhibits, and programs, the museum tells its story about people of the past through the re-creation of everyday life down to its smallest details.

"Every individual," wrote Harriet Beecher Stowe, one of rural New England's great chroniclers, "is part and parcel of a great picture of the society in which he lives and acts, and his life cannot be painted without reproducing a picture of the world he lived in." To present that picture is the abiding mission of Old Sturbridge Village. Central also to this mission are the museum's extensive holdings of some 100,000 objects of everyday life, all of them made or used in New England in the early years of the American republic. Bringing together extraordinary collections, creative research, and dynamic interpretation, the Village provides a powerful, personal encounter with the past—not only its people, ideas, and events, but its sights, sounds, smells, and textures.

One of the museum's greatest strengths is its collection of textiles, which represents in remarkable detail what early New Englanders wore and used in their homes. Among that collection's treasures is an important and highly representative group of nearly 250 New England quilts dating between the late eighteenth and the mid-nineteenth centuries. With the publication of *Northern Comfort: New England's Early Quilts 1780-1850*, Old Sturbridge Village has an opportunity to share many of these remarkable quilts and to tell the compelling story of how and why they were designed and made.

In the years spanned by this book, rural New England was poised between the ways of tradition and the opportunities presented by economic and technological change. Ranging from the everyday to the elegantly beautiful, from the seemingly simple to the strikingly complex, these quilts are the visible reflections of those rapidly changing times. This book has drawn on the Village's artifact and library collections, the scholarship of a talented curator and the museum's chief historian, and the creativity and energy of the museum's publications team.

Old Sturbridge Village takes great pride in presenting *Northern Comfort* as part of a "great picture of society," celebrating the artistry, ingenuity, and extraordinary needlecraft of early New England's quilts and the women who made them.

Alberta Sebolt George
PRESIDENT
OLD STURBRIDGE VILLAGE

Acknowledgments

Northern Comfort is the result of an extensive collaboration and the generous sharing of resources of Old Sturbridge Village staff, past and present. Mark Ashton and Doris Mittasch provided editorial assistance for the publication. Stacia Caplanson assisted with fact-checking and research during the writing process. Old Sturbridge Village volunteers Paul Baran, Vivian Chapin, Beth Marie Forrest, Judy Knight, and Sandra Skala provided quilt research assistance.

The museum also extends its gratitude to the Colonial Williamsburg Foundation, the Connecticut Historical Society, the Henry Francis Du Pont Winterthur Museum, the Shelburne Museum, the Society for the Preservation of New England Antiquities, the Victoria and Albert Museum, the Wadsworth Atheneum, the Webb-Deane-Stevens Museum, and the Welsh Folk Museum, for making their quilt collections accessible for study and sharing research information.

Old Sturbridge Village is particularly grateful to Larry Stone and John Mitchell of Rutledge Hill Press for helping to make *Northern Comfort* a reality, bringing these remarkable quilts and their stories to a wider audience, and to Harriette Bateman of Bateman Design for designing the book and jacket.

Special thanks go to the Quilter's Guild of Dallas, for a grant helping to support the preparation of this book.

About *Northern Comfort*

Lynne Z. Bassett, Curator of Textiles and Fine Arts at Old Sturbridge Village, holds degrees from Mount Holyoke College and the University of Connecticut. She was responsible for the research and analysis—in textile collections, documents, and quilt scholarship—that went into *Northern Comfort*. Lynne also has authored articles and essays and is a frequent lecturer on textiles of early America.

Jack Larkin, the museum's chief historian and Director of Research, Collections, and Library, has also authored numerous articles and books, including the award-winning *The Reshaping of Everyday Life: 1790-1840*. Joining the museum in 1971 with degrees from Harvard College and Brandeis University, he has played a critical role in bringing the museum's scholarship to its diverse public audience, interpreting the history of the "everyday, ordinary" people that might otherwise be forgotten.

Award-winning Museum Photographer Thomas Neill is the primary photographer for the Village's publications. Tom was responsible for the preponderance of the photography for *Northern Comfort*, with additional photographs by Henry Peach and Anna D. Shaw.

Northern COMFORT

New England's Early Quilts

1 7 8 0 - 1 8 5 0

Gathering Up the Fragments

"The true economy of housekeeping," wrote Lydia Maria Child, "is simply the art of gathering up all the fragments, so that nothing be lost. I mean fragments of *time*, as well as *materials*."[1] Child's *The American Frugal Housewife*, published in 1833, became a kind of domestic Bible for New England women. In it, she echoed Scripture in a way that all her readers would recognize. They would catch the familiar words from John's Gospel, from the story of the loaves and fishes. It was the Lord's command to "gather up the fragments that remain, that nothing be lost." These words are a key to understanding New England quilts and quilting. Dozens of diaries and thousands of pieces of needlework tell us that New England women in the early nineteenth century took this instruction to heart, filling the spare moments in their days with the production of necessary and often beautiful items for their homes and families.

"GATHER UP the fragments that remain, that nothing be lost."

Bed quilts particularly embodied the biblical injunction to "gather up the fragments," for by the nineteenth century, they were often made of bits of worn-out clothing and furnishing fabrics, and scraps remaining from the creation of new clothing. Constructed of many different fabrics and organized in repeating blocks, New England's pieced or "patchwork" quilts reflected the reality of women's lives. Just as they stitched calicoes, women pieced together the

PLATE 1. *Miniature-pieced quilt of printed cottons, c. 1840, attributed to Susannah Allen Anderson Howard (1813-1891) of Ware, Massachusetts.*

disparate tasks of cooking, cleaning, caring for children, gardening, dairying, sewing, knitting, and washing for their families.

So, too, quilt collectors and historians have gathered up surviving New England quilts and pieced together fragments of evidence about their makers. This book celebrates the artistry and variety of these quilts, and also attempts to reconstruct the history of their development and their significance in society, both to the people who made them and to us. It draws on the work of those collectors and historians, on quilts that have been published, and on quilts that have been made accessible by museums and individuals.

Northern Comfort's most important sources are threefold. First is the quilt collection at Old Sturbridge Village, nearly 250 New England quilts dating from the 1780s to the 1850s. With its remarkable range and depth, this collection provides examples of virtually every style and material used in early New England quilting and documents the actual practices of New England quilters. The second is an illuminating group of New England women's diaries, both published and manuscript, spanning the years from 1767 to 1850. These records have been intensively studied for their descriptions of quilts and quilting. The third is Old Sturbridge Village itself as an outdoor museum of living history. The Village's extensive programs of research, interpretation, and demonstration in the social and material history of early New England provide a unique vantage point, and unparalleled resources, for this book.

The story of quilts in New England goes back in some ways to the seventeenth century. But to understand the New England women who made them, the best place to start might be with Susannah Allen Anderson Howard of Ware, Massachusetts. Born in 1813 and orphaned in 1827, Susannah Anderson, along with her two younger brothers, became the ward of an uncle but soon came to live in the farming household of her widowed grandfather, William Anderson. William, who had been a soldier in the Revolutionary War, must have welcomed the help, for at the age of fourteen Susannah would surely have been competent at cooking, housekeeping, and sewing. She was undoubtedly already accustomed to the demanding labor of maintaining a household and feeding a family; her father would have relied heavily on Susannah's help for housekeeping and child care during the two years following her mother's death and preceding his own. [2]

As Susannah advanced to young womanhood, her life did not get easier. Another uncle died, leaving six more orphans for her extended family to care for, and then her grandfather and finally her guardian died, leaving Susannah with the guardianship of her brothers. Long before her marriage, she had acquired domestic skills, borne heavy responsibilities, and experienced more than her share of illness and death.

Susannah's early years were difficult but not really unusual in a world where medical care was often ineffective and there were stark limits on life expectancy. She went on to be a wife and mother who lived a responsible and caring life, but Susannah was not remarkable—except for what she left behind. She was a quilter of genuine skill and originality. Two quilts can be attributed to her, each passed down through a different branch of her descendants. One is an astonishing miniature-pieced quilt of approximately twelve thousand pieces, as intricate, multicolored, and finely wrought as a tile mosaic [Plate 1]. The other is very different, a "whitework" bed quilt with a knotted fringe, whose beauty lies in the subtle elegance of its design [Plate 2].

Given the course of her life, it is doubtful that Susannah had the opportunity for education beyond her town's district schools. Yet her quilts show that she possessed an active mind, an interest in technical challenges, a powerful aesthetic sense, and patience. In 1839 Susannah married Emery Howard, who had come to town from Vermont, and they settled on their own farm in Ware. As many women did, Susannah may well have made the quilts for her new household, using her skills for the first time in her own home. We can imagine that she thoroughly enjoyed the opportunity.

Susannah's rural community of Ware, Massachusetts, owed its growth and prosperity to the dramatic changes wrought by the Industrial Revolution that was sweeping across New England in the early nineteenth century. Settled in the second quarter of the eighteenth century, Ware struggled as a poor farming

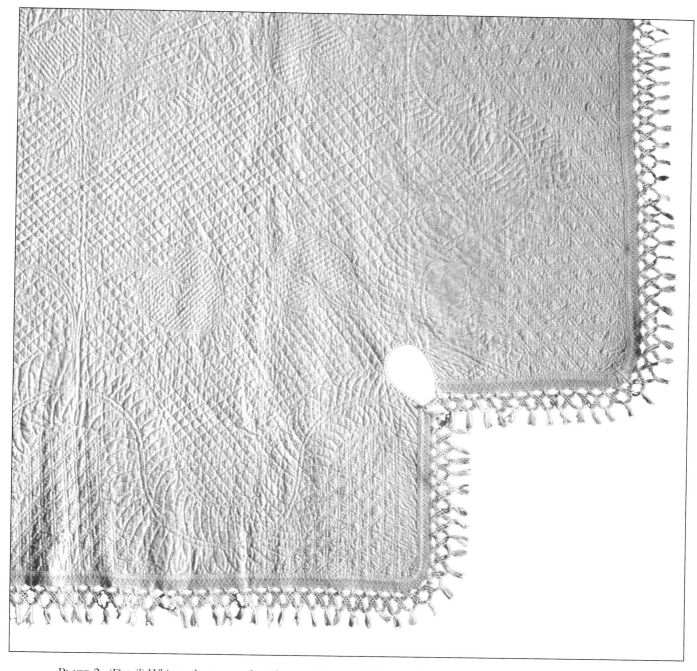

PLATE 2. *(Detail) Whitework cotton quilt with cotton fringe, c. 1840, made by Susannah Anderson Howard (1813-1891) of Ware, Massachusetts.*

community for three generations until the water power of the Ware River was harnessed by textile mills in the 1820s. By the late 1830s, the center of the town had shifted a mile east, away from the original meetinghouse, to the "factory village." Young women and some families from Ware, surrounding towns, and many places farther away came to work in the mills, tending spinning throstles and power looms. In 1837, two years before Susannah's marriage, the mills in Ware turned out nearly two million yards of cotton and woolen cloth.[3]

Susannah's quilts were also products of the Industrial Revolution. In the eighteenth century, the cotton cloth and colorful printed designs used to make the miniature-pieced quilt would have been expensive imported fabrics, woven and block-printed by hand, and far beyond the means of a woman from a modest rural household. By the early nineteenth century the enormous success of factory spinning, weaving, and cylinder printing—in both New England and Britain—had dramatically reduced the price of cotton cloth and brought a multitude of new fabrics within the reach of the great majority of American families.

Especially after 1820, this new profusion of colors and patterns was visible everywhere in households and in everyday clothing. It encouraged the making of pieced quilts, because fabrics and scraps were now abundant, and inspired women to create scores of innovative quilt block designs. Susannah's miniature-pieced quilt, with its central medallion of mosaic patchwork and intricate layers of block-pieced borders, with fifteen different designs, is a remarkable blend of tradition and innovation. It strikingly illustrates the transition in New England quiltmaking in the first half of the nineteenth century from a conventional British design to one that was recognizably American.

Susannah's whitework quilt links her not to the rural vernacular but to the Neoclassical taste of the early nineteenth century and the multiple ironies of mechanization. It is a skillful, hand-stitched emulation of a bedcover of Marseilles quilting—a widely popular textile that was machine-produced on Jacquard looms. Marseilles quilting itself had been created in imitation of

PLATE 3. *"South-western view of Ware Village," woodcut by J. W. Barber and A. Gilmore, 1839. The new textile factory buildings along the Ware River can be seen at the right. [John Warner Barber,* Massachusetts Historical Collections *(Worcester, Mass.: Dorr and Howland, 1840), 343.]*

traditional handwork from the Provence region of France. Whitework quilts were genteel, approved by urban makers of taste and arbiters of fashion, in a way that pieced calico quilts, even one as vibrantly original as Susannah's, were not.

Like other New England women of her time, Susannah Anderson Howard was both drawn to the rural vernacular and aspired to fashion and gentility. In many respects, hers is the story of New England quilting.

ENDNOTES

1. Lydia Maria Child, *The American Frugal Housewife* (Boston: Carter, Hendee and Babcock, 1833), 1.
2. Susannah Allen Anderson Howard's story and that of her family were gathered from: the probate records of Hampshire County, Box 275 #8; Box 4 #59; Box 319 #15, Hall of Records, Northampton, Mass.; manuscript schedules of the Federal Censuses of Population for Massachusetts, 1820, 1830, 1840, 1850, microfilm at the Old Sturbridge Village Research Library; Arthur Chase, *History of Ware, Massachusetts* (Cambridge, Mass.: The University Press, 1911); Jay Mack Holbrook, comp., *Vital Records for the Town of Ware, Massachusetts, 1735-1893* (Jay Mack Holbrook: Oxford, Mass., 1983) microfiche.
3. John Warner Barber, *Massachusetts Historical Collections* (Worcester, Mass.: Dorr and Howland, 1840), 343.

Chapter I

Twisted Some Worsted for Quilting

Whole Cloth Quilts of the Seventeenth, Eighteenth, and Early Nineteenth Centuries

New England's Earliest Quilts

The romantic historians of the late nineteenth and early twentieth centuries have created an enduringly sentimental vision of early New England quilting. From the beginnings of settlement, they assumed, New England women could be found frugally piecing quilts from bits of leftover cloth—both to keep their families warm during bitterly cold winters and to relieve the austerity of sparsely furnished houses with a spot of color and beauty. This is an attractive vision but not an accurate one.

Quilts of any kind were very rare in New England in the seventeenth and early eighteenth centuries, and it is unlikely that New England women were making quilts in any number until at least the 1750s. All of the evidence indicates that the great majority of quilts on early American beds during this period were expensive imported items, a few from India but most of them from England, where they were commercially made by the upholstery trade.

QUILTS OF ANY kind were rare in New England in the seventeenth century.

As New England women began to make their own quilts, they worked in the dominant English quilting tradition of their time. They did not produce pieced or patchwork quilts but "whole cloth" quilts made of a single fabric— wool or silk. These quilts were not inexpensive alternatives to wool blankets or other bed coverings but instead were items of conspicuous display and symbols of wealth.[1]

A quilt that once belonged to Catherine Colepepper (afterward Lady Fairfax) of Virginia, is perhaps the only surviving example known to have been owned in seventeenth-century America. It exemplifies luxury and symbolizes wealth. It is made of hand-spun white Indian cotton, then a rarity, and is embroidered in yellow silk with designs of vines and flowers, human figures, unusual animals, winged mermaids, and other fantastic creatures.[2] It was an exotic import from Bengal in India, an item of high value and prestige.

No documented seventeenth-century bed quilt survives from New England, but there are scattered references to quilts as household possessions in the wills and estate inventories of the wealthy. The earliest quilt in New England for which we have a record was a "fflock bed quilt" owned by Samuel Fuller of Plymouth Colony in 1633. Despite the inelegant description that focused on its stuffing ("flock" was coarse wool or chopped-up fabrics used as wadding in quilted clothing and bed quilts, and as stuffing for beds), Fuller's quilt was an expensive item, assessed at more than twice the value of the household's "white ruggs" (heavy tufted bedcovers) or wool blankets.[3]

Most of these earliest New England quilts were constructed of wool or silk in solid colors. Some were, like Catherine Colepepper's, made of costly Indian cotton, although none of them seem to have been embroidered; some were instead made of hand-decorated calico, a brightly colored and patterned fabric named for the western port of Calicut (now Calcutta). At the time of his death in 1685, the merchant George Corwin of Salem, Massachusetts, owned three "white quilts," which might have been of either wool or silk, and "1 quilt of calico Colered & flowred." Each was worth between one and two pounds sterling, a substantial sum.[4]

In the early years of the eighteenth century, quilts, as documented in wills and inventories, were more abundant in New England, although they were still rare, confined to prosperous households. London upholsterers—whose trade had grown to significant size by producing the elaborate bed hangings that were fashionable in the seventeenth and eighteenth centuries—employed professional quilters to supply bed quilts for affluent families in both England and America. *The London Tradesman* of 1747 noted that these male master quilters, with their meagerly paid female helpers, made quilted petticoats as well as "quilts for beds." Their work was "nothing to get rich by," except for those few who could purchase their own materials and sell their quilts independently. [5]

One of the earliest references to the making of quilts in New England is an advertisement in the *Boston News-Letter* for August 20, 1716. The widow and daughters of George Brownell, who had kept a private school, advertised that their establishment would undertake quilting and "all sorts of Millinary works...making up Dresses...the cutting of Gentlewomens Hair in the newest Fashion..." along with teaching dancing and many kinds of fine needlework. This may well have been the way a quilting tradition began in New England—through the quilts made and the instruction offered by professional needlewomen like the Brownells, who presumably had learned from English examples. Gradually, the quilts on New England beds became a mix of imported pieces and ones made locally of (for the face at least) imported fabrics.[6]

In merchants' advertisements, there is abundant evidence of the continuing importation of English quilts in a variety of colors and sizes until the American Revolution. In 1760 a Boston merchant advertised that he had on hand "6, 7, 8, 9 & 10 qr Bed Quilts"—that is, quilts that ranged in width from "six quarters" of a yard (1.5 yards or 54 inches) to "ten quarters" of a yard (2.5 yards or 90 inches). [7] Most surviving eighteenth-century New England quilts are made of "calamanco," a fabric woven from tightly spun, high-quality worsted wool, favored for its long, lustrous fibers. Calamanco had a smooth, shiny finish produced by "calendering," or pressing the cloth between hot metal plates. These calendered wool fabrics came in a variety of weaves, including plain, satin, and twill, as well as striped and brocaded flower patterns, all of which appear in early New England whole cloth quilts.[8] The most frequently seen color in calamanco quilts is dark blue, followed by bright pink, but surviving quilts can also be found in deep purple, green, yellow, red, and brown.

The aesthetic appeal of whole cloth quilts came not, of course, in their combinations of color and pattern, but in the designs created by the quilting stitches themselves. The gloss of shiny fabrics such as silk or calamanco heightened the effect of the quilting design. For the earliest New England quilts that survive, these quilting designs are often quite elaborate, with remarkable scrolling feathers and

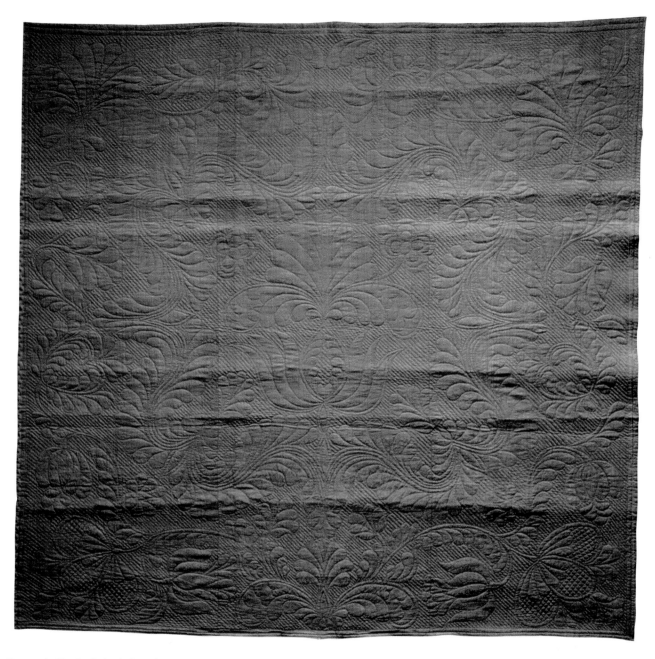

PLATE 4. *Wool whole cloth quilt, c. 1760-1800. Backed with a glazed pink wool, this quilt may have been imported from England, as eighteenth-century English quilted petticoats often use the same type of plain-woven glazed wool fabric for a lining. The design of the quilting is very sophisticated, with a central focus on a stylized floral motif, surrounded by S-curved feathers. The S-curve, called "the line of beauty," is typical of the rococo style. The original green color of the quilt face is now much faded.*

imaginative foliate motifs. These undulating figures imitated the rococo curves fashionable in high-style English and American furniture, and closely resemble the stylized floral designs embroidered on bed hangings and woven into the silk fabrics of fashionable clothing for both men and women. From the late eighteenth century on, these elaborate quilted designs often gave way to geometric diamond lattices and simpler swagged feather motifs—a change that probably reflects the simplified lines of the newly dominant Neoclassical style.

Quilted Petticoats

Quilted petticoats, often referred to as "quilts" or "coats" in diaries, as distinct from "bed quilts," became important items of women's dress in the middle decades of the eighteenth century, when, sometimes elaborately stitched, they were displayed under the open-fronted skirts of fashionable gowns. While women could buy imported quilted petticoats as well as bed quilts from merchants in Boston and other cities, it seems likely that an increasing number of them chose to make their own, looking for affordable fashion.

PLATE 5. *Quilted calamanco petticoat, c. 1760-1790, probably made in New England.*

It is entirely possible, in fact, that the fashion for quilted petticoats generated the first major surge in home quilting activity. Petticoats at first predominated in what New England quilters produced. Between 1767 and 1777—the first ten years documented by the New England quilters' diaries examined for this book—diary keepers recorded three days working on quilted petticoats to every one spent on bed quilts. By the turn of the century, elaborate quilted petticoats fell out of common use, when the slim lines of the Neoclassical style made them unfashionably bulky. Petticoats returned to favor (and began to be mentioned once more in quilters' diaries) when skirts filled out again in the 1820s—but this time they served for warmth rather than style.

New England Characteristics

The importation of English quilts slowed and then ceased during the last quarter of the eighteenth century. First, the American Revolution broke the bonds of commerce and encouraged the use of domestic textiles. Then, after the war, quilt manufacturing in London itself declined, as the fashions for whole cloth quilts, as well as quilted petticoats, passed in England. [9]

Many New England-made whole cloth quilts have a face of calamanco or other fine-quality imported wool and a backing (often called a "lining" by early quilters) of more coarsely woven wool, sometimes homespun and home-woven. In their weight and texture many of these backings closely resemble surviving early home-woven wool sheets. On a few quilts the remnants of cross-stitched initials—with which household linens and undergarments were often marked—indicate the careful recycling of old textiles.

These quilt backings are also very frequently a distinctive golden yellow color. The "most esteemed" quilts, noted Elizabeth H. Rollins of rural New Hampshire, "were lined with yellow." [10] Sarah Snell Bryant of Cummington, Massachusetts, in 1817, and Mary Avery White of Boylston, Massachusetts, in 1840, noted specifically that they had dyed, or "colored," their bed quilt linings yellow. It has been traditionally thought that these yellow wool fabrics had been dyed with butternut bark, but early dye recipes tell us instead that butternut was used to create "a very

PLATE 6.
Quilted silk petticoat, c. 1820-1840, from the Seabury family of Little Compton, Rhode Island. It is not unusual for quilted petticoats of this period to have shoulder straps to help bear the garment's weight.

PLATE 7. *Whole cloth calamanco quilt, New England. The maker of this quilt, who incorporated her initials, "A D," and the year, 1789, into her quilting, had some trouble laying out her quilting pattern at the corners. Rather than making a smoothly turning curve, the pattern of an undulating "feather" is simply overlapped. This quilt is lined with a plain-woven yellow wool. The binding is a later addition.*

PLATE 8. *Spinning wool on the "great wheel" or "walking wheel" at Old Sturbridge Village.*

handsome dark brown equal to a good London mud."[11] New England quilters may have achieved their yellow with "fustic," a dye wood imported from South America, as most published dye recipes suggested, or a number of vegetable dyes.

However, Lydia Maria Child's *American Frugal Housewife* offered a specific recipe for a yellow dye that was "very useful for the linings of bed-quilts, comforters, &c." She told her readers that "A pailful of lye, with a piece of copperas half as big as a hen's egg boiled in it, will color a fine nankin [yellow] color, which will never wash out."[12] Copperas was a dyestuff made from iron, and lye referred to the strong-smelling "chamber lye," stale urine valued for its ammonia, which many New England households still kept available to use for dyeing. Golden yellow may well have been the color most often chosen for quilt linings precisely because it was so easy to obtain; but it also hid dirt well and—as Child claimed and surviving examples attest—it did not fade much with washing.

New England quilts were sometimes also distinctive in their shape. Quilts made in the region dating from the late eighteenth through the nineteenth century occasionally can be found that are constructed in a "T" shape, rather than in the usual square or rectangular form. This shape—essentially unknown outside the region—has a practical purpose. It accommodates the posts of a bedstead, allowing a quilt to lie smoothly without "bunching up" around the foot posts. [13]

"…[T]wisted some worsted for quilting…," wrote Sarah Snell Bryant in 1824. The stitches that both decorate New England wool quilts and hold their layers together are almost always made of a two-ply worsted wool thread, probably hand-spun. Even in 1837, when factory-made thread was readily available, Pamela Brown of Plymouth, Vermont, noted that "Mrs. Wilder spun me some worsted to quilt with." In most quilts, the color of the thread was chosen to blend with the fabric on the face, but sometimes women used quilting thread in a contrasting color, perhaps in a conscious effort to make their designs stand out more clearly.

The last step in making a quilt, after it had been cut off the quilting frame,

PLATE 9. *(Detail) Whole cloth wool quilt, 1795, made by Mary Hill Nowell of New Hampshire. The quilt is finished with a home-woven twill wool binding.*

was to finish the raw edges of the fabric. It has been argued by British quilt historians that it was a typically American, as distinct from English, practice to bind quilts—that is, finish their edges with a sewn-on cloth tape.[14] Actually, this did not become a common practice in New England until the rise of cotton quilts in the nineteenth century and was never widely found in woolen quilts. Most New England whole cloth quilts are finished with a "knife edge," in which the raw edges of both the face and backing fabrics are tucked in and then secured by a running stitch. Binding is much less common, although it does occasionally appear and is occasionally mentioned by diarists. Mary Hill Nowell of New Hampshire, who has been credited by family tradition with raising the sheep, spinning the yarn, and weaving the fabric for her 1795 wool whole cloth quilt, used a home-woven twill tape of green wool to finish its edges [Plate 9].

Batting was the least visible part of any quilt, but it too has a history. Inside surviving whole cloth quilts there is usually a batting of carded wool. It is not unusual to find that the wool batting of a whole cloth quilt has itself been dyed. Some quilts with dark-colored faces (for example, the green wool quilt in Plate 4) have battings that are dyed blue or are made from the naturally dark wool of black sheep. Here quilters were solving an otherwise troubling aesthetic problem. Stitching a quilt inevitably pulled some batting fibers through to the surface; dark-colored fibers would not show up to mar the design. More rarely, a quilter chose to have the batting of a light-colored quilt dyed to match, as is the case with a yellow whole cloth wool quilt in the collection of the Shelburne Museum in Vermont. [15]

Sometimes the face and backing of a bed quilt hides a batting made of materials that its maker would not have wanted anyone to see—poorly dyed wool and otherwise unusable material, probably what would have been considered "flock" batting. A red wool whole cloth quilt from New Hampshire provides an example; its batting is made up of light wool, dark wool, cotton, and the short, dark fibers of linen called "tow," all carded together. After water-powered machine carding of wool became widely available in New England around 1810, the quality of battings undoubtedly improved. [16] However, some women continued to card their quilt battings by hand. Sarah Snell Bryant noted

PLATE 10. *Wool is processed by the roll card (foreground) and batt card in the Hapgood Carding Mill at Old Sturbridge Village. After 1800, hundreds of such rural mills provided New England households with roving for spinning and batting for quilts and comforters.*

several times between 1810 and 1834 that she "…carded wool for a bedquilt…."

Cotton batting, although used in quilts imported from India in the seventeenth century, was too valuable to use inside New England–made quilts until the growth of New England's textile industry in the early nineteenth century made it cheap indeed. By the 1830s, merchants' advertisements tell us that it cost a few cents a pound and could be bought by the bale. As the Scottish observer James Montgomery noted in 1840, the "inferior waste" of cotton manufacturing was made "into what is called batting" and then "rolled up in paper for the purpose of being sold to country people" who used it in the making of quilts.[17] The appearance of a cotton batting in a wool whole cloth quilt dates it to the early nineteenth century and provides strong evidence of this traditional form's longevity in New England.

An Enduring Tradition

When pieced-block designs became popular for cotton bed quilts in the early nineteenth century, some New England quilters adapted the new designs for use in traditional wool whole cloth quilts. They took the lines of geometrically pieced blocks and translated them into quilting patterns. Many wool whole cloth quilts from the years after 1800 are quilted in designs resembling the geometric blocks of early pieced cotton quilts: designs of squares "on point" (turned to create a diamond shape) with bands of "sashing" separating each, and often with flower, heart, or quatrefoil motifs quilted within them.

The growing fashion for pieced-block cotton quilts affected the design of wool quilts in another way. Some late eighteenth- and early nineteenth-century quilters continued the tradition of working in wool but made pieced quilts whose designs, using contrasting colors, were similar to early examples of block patchwork in cotton. Star designs were popular among the makers of these pieced wool quilts; a particularly good example can be seen in the red and green wool quilt pictured in Plate 11. In 1830 Sarah Snell Bryant made a pieced wool quilt that must have been striking in its effect. She described it in her diary as "…worsted red and black, the wide red border pieced."

Sarah began early to make "patchwork" and "pieced" bed quilts, commenting on them in her diary from the time she started keeping it in 1794. But a notation as late as 1834 about making "a thick cloth bed quilt" indicates that she was still making whole cloth quilts as well. ("Cloth" was a term often used to describe a wool fabric, and a "thick" wool fabric could not easily have been used for a pieced design.)

PLATE 11. *Pieced wool quilt, c. 1820-1830, New England. The wool fringe decorating the edges of this quilt is original.*

PLATE 12. *Pieced wool quilt, c. 1800-1825, Wellfleet, Massachusetts. The maker used a dramatic variation of a strip-pieced design.*

Other New England quilters continued to produce whole cloth quilts in the 1830s and early 1840s; their diaries refer to washing wool quilts, spinning worsted thread for quilting, and dyeing wool quilt linings. Wool and worsted quilts continued to be listed on probate inventories through the 1840s. Beginning as fashionable and expensive imports, whole cloth wool quilts persisted as an enduring tradition of the New England countryside.

ENDNOTES

1. Sally Garoutte, "Early Colonial Quilts in a Bedding Context," *Uncoverings … 1980 … Research Papers of the American Quilt Study Group*, vol. 1, (Mill Valley, Calif., 1981), 18-27.
2. Accession number 1987-551, collection of Colonial Williamsburg Foundation, Williamsburg, Va.
3. "Plymouth Colony Wills and Inventories," *The Mayflower Descendant*, 2, no. 1 (January 1950): 8-10. Fuller owned "a fflock bed quilt & bolster." This reference has been interpreted variously by quilt scholars; see Garoutte, "Early Colonial Quilts," and Nancy Halpern, exhibit notes for "The Wool Quilts of New England," courtesy of the New England Quilt Museum, Lowell, Mass. It was the general practice until well into the nineteenth century to refer to a quilt as a "bed quilt," to differentiate it from quilted clothing; also, the assessors of Fuller's personal property consistently denoted individual items within a group by designating "a handsaw," "a pickaxe," "a churn." Therefore it is here assumed that they were describing a flock bed quilt, not a flock bed and a quilt. While nine items consisting of three "white ruggs," (heavy, tufted wool bed covers) and three pairs of blankets were valued together at one pound (twenty shillings), the "fflock bed quilt & bolster" together were worth proportionately much more at ten shillings.
4. Quoted in Garoutte, "Early Colonial Quilts," 26.
5. Quoted in Janet Rae, *The Quilts of the British Isles* (New York: E. P. Dutton, 1987), 18.
6. George Francis Dow, *The Arts & Crafts in New England*, 1704-1775 (Topsfield, Mass.: The Wayside Press, 1927), 273.
7. Dow, 170.
8. Hazel Cummins, "Calamanco," *The Magazine Antiques*, 39, no. 4 (April 1941): 182-184. In the eighteenth century the term seems to have been reserved for satin weaves.
9. Dorothy Osler, *Traditional British Quilts* (London: B. T. Batsford, 1987), 95.
10. Ellen H. Rollins, *New England Bygones* (Philadelphia: J. B. Lippincott & Co., 1883), 237.
11. J. & R. Bronson, *The Domestic Manufacturer's Assistant, and Family Directory in the Arts of Weaving and Dyeing* (Utica, N.Y.: William Williams, 1817), 191.
12. Lydia Maria Child, *The American Frugal Housewife* (Boston: Carter, Hendee and Babcock, 1833), 39.
13. Jeanette Lasansky, "T-Shaped Quilts: A New England Phenomenon," *The Magazine Antiques* 152, no. 6 (December 1997): 842-845.
14. Janet Rae, et al. *Quilt Treasures of Great Britain, The Heritage Search of the Quilters' Guild* (Nashville: Rutledge Hill Press, 1995), 120.
15. Accession number 10-275, collection of Shelburne Museum, Shelburne, Vt.
16. The Secretary of the Treasury reported in 1810 that almost every New England town with a population of 200 families had a carding mill: Albert Gallatin, "Report on Manufactures," *American State Papers: Documents, Legislative and Executive* (38 vols., Washington, 1832-1861), Finance II, 435. See also Barnes Riznik, "New England Wool-Carding and Finishing Mills, 1790-1840," unpublished research report, Old Sturbridge Village, 1964, 1-2.
17. *Massachusetts Spy* (Worcester), January 1, 1834, 1; James Montgomery, *A Practical Detail of the Cotton Manufacture of the United States of America* (Glasgow, 1840), 49.

Chapter II

Patchwork Is Good Economy

Quilting Becomes a Democratic Art

The Beginnings of Patchwork

The art of making patchwork quilts came to America from England where it had a history dating back at least to the beginning of the eighteenth century. At that time, and for some years to come, "patchwork" had a quite specific meaning; it signified a pieced mosaic design created by the repetition of a single geometrical shape, such as a square or a hexagon. (Later, in nineteenth-century America, "patchwork" and "pieced" came to be essentially equivalent terms.) Mosaic patchwork was created by cutting pieces of cloth approximately to shape, basting them over carefully prepared paper templates, and then using a whip stitch to sew the shapes together, edge-to-edge. After the top was finished, the papers were usually removed. The fashion for patchwork quilts does not seem to have come to America until the 1770s, when the first written references to them appear.[1] The earliest surviving American example dates from 1785.

THE FASHION FOR patchwork does not seem to have come to America until the 1770s.

In 1774, a gentleman of Boston, James Otis, bequeathed to his daughter Hannah "…both her patch work Counterpens that she made herself…."[2] Mosaic patchwork quilting in New England almost certainly began as a genteel accomplishment for well-to-do young ladies, who received instruction in fancy needlework as part of their education. Eleanor Druitt taught privileged girls like Hannah Otis; in the *Boston News-Letter* of 1771 she listed quilting as one of the

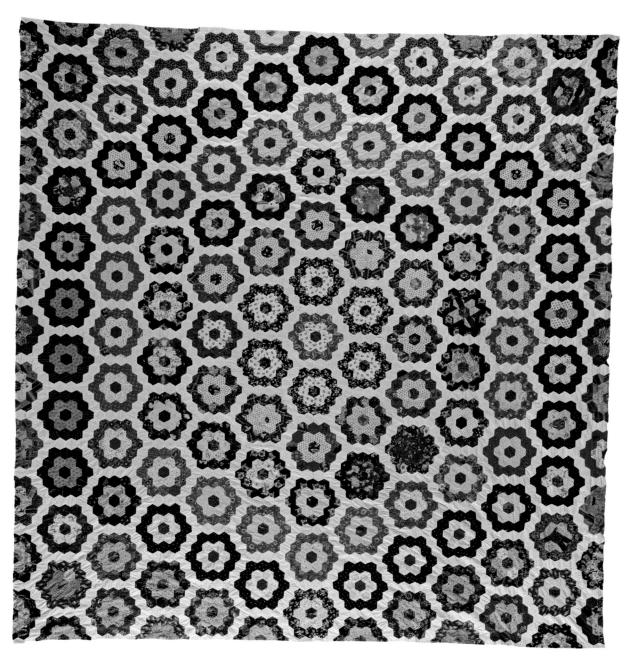

PLATE 13. *Hexagon mosaic template-pieced quilt top of printed cottons, c. 1835-1840.*

PLATE 14. *(Detail) Hexagon mosaic template-pieced quilt top of printed cottons, c. 1830. The papers were not removed from this unfinished quilt.*

forms of needlework she was prepared to teach, along with others that ranged from "Sprigging, Embroidery, Cat-Gut, [and] Diaper" to "Marking, Plain Work, and Knitting." [3]

Perhaps the earliest documented example of American patchwork is a wool bed quilt believed to be from Maine and dated 1785 in an appliquéd inscription. Now in the collection of the Wadsworth Atheneum in Hartford, Connecticut, it was a gift to a young woman, identified by its full inscription: "ANNA TUELS HER BEDqUILT GIVEN TO HER BY HER MOTHER IN THE YEAR AU 23. 1785." Its maker—presumably Mrs. Tuels—created a mosaic design of squares within a broad border of pink calamanco. Each square is created from four template-pieced wool triangles, whose paper linings remain inside the quilt.

With its beginnings in the late eighteenth century, the mosaic patchwork tradition grew and flourished in New England in the years after 1800, making its way from the households of the highly prosperous to more middling families. Template-pieced mosaic quilts from the 1820s and 1830s illustrate fidelity to English tradition in design, although they are constructed in large part from factory-made and machine-printed cotton fabrics [Plate 13]. One example in the Old Sturbridge Village collection, dated around 1830, documents the construction of a quilt in process. It is a quilt top that was never joined to its backing, and its still-attached paper templates can be clearly seen [Plate 14].

Chintz Appliqué

Quilts decorated with appliqué work of cut-out chintz represented another quilting style that came from fashionable English households to prosperous American ones in the last quarter of the eighteenth century and then became more democratically widespread in the nineteenth. Today this style is known as *broderie perse* ("Persian embroidery"), a term coined in the late nineteenth century. Quilters cut out individual images or motifs from printed fabrics, then rearranged them to form large-scale designs that they stitched onto plain, usually white, backings. Early in the popularity of *broderie perse*, many quiltmakers cut

PLATE 15. *Cut-out chintz appliqué quilt of plain and printed cottons, Tree of Life design, c. 1820. The stripes and medallions seen in the inner borders of this quilt were printed especially for use in appliqué work.*

out their appliquéd figures from pieces of costly hand-block-printed and painted Indian cotton chintz, a fabric with a "glazed," or smooth and shiny, surface. They were also able to use glazed English and French printed cottons—a little less expensive but still costly—whose block-printed or copperplate-printed images were often inspired by the exotic Indian originals.

During the first quarter of the nineteenth century, the fashion for cut-out chintz appliqué was reaching many middling families, moving well beyond the confines of elite households and costly materials. English textile manufacturers began to print relatively inexpensive fabrics with motifs designed especially for such work after about 1815. Both continuity of style and change in materials are evident in a New England cut-out chintz appliqué quilt, dating from around 1820 [Plate 15]. Its design—a central flowering tree called the "Tree of Life," surrounded by a colorful border, is the one most frequently used by English and American quilters. The Tree of Life design was inspired by the figures seen on Indian "palampores," elaborately painted and expensive cotton bedcovers that had been exported to England since the seventeenth century.

PLATE 16. *"The Calico Printer," woodcut illustrating the block printing of textiles by hand. Not pictured is the printer's assistant who applied the dye or "color" to the block. This work was slow and painstaking because the blocks printed only one section at a time and needed to be carefully aligned to ensure proper execution of the design.* [The Book of English Trades *(London: Printed for C. and J. Rivington, 1827), facing page 66.*]

From Scarcity to Abundance

Through most of the eighteenth century, these patchworked and appliquéd quilts graced the bed chambers of the economic elite, as only the wealthy could afford the expensive, elaborately produced fabrics that went into their creation. They still represented a world in which fabrics had not yet become cheap and abundant. From cleaning and combing or carding, through spinning and weaving, to finishing and decorating, textiles could be produced only by arduous and often exacting hand labor. Cloth, in all its forms, was expensive because of the days and weeks of work it embodied, and textiles accounted for a very large proportion of the value of household possessions.

PLATE 17. *"Calico Printing," engraving illustrating the cylinder printing of textiles. The printing cylinder is visible at the front of the machine to the right. The cylinder passed through a trough of "color" or dye immediately below it, filling up its engraved lines; the excess was scraped off by a steel blade mounted against it. The fabric yardage (which could be miles long) received its printed design as it was drawn across the engraved cylinder by the larger working cylinder just above it. [George S. White,* Memoir of Samuel Slater *(Philadelphia: 46 Carpenter St., 1836), facing page 395.]*

As a consequence, housewives in ordinary families found fabric too expensive to use liberally. The yardage for window curtains or bed hangings was calculated so closely that there was no allowance made for matching the fabric's pattern at the seams. Clothing was likewise cut as efficiently as possible, often using patterns based on variations of squares, rectangles, and triangles, so that there was little fabric left over. Not only were new fabrics expensive, but scrap bags in the great majority of households did not yield an inspiring selection of fragments to "gather up" into interesting patchwork designs!

Rural merchants' account books from the 1780s and 1790s reveal that this equation still held true in New England. "Fine chintz" cost between $1.00 and $1.25 per yard, while good quality calico cost about $1.10.[4] A farm laborer at this time would have made about 50¢ per day, and a skilled artisan no more than $1.00; so that a single yard of either of these fabrics would have cost between one and two days' wages.

However, the Industrial Revolution was already underway in England, a process that would transform the world of textiles from scarcity to abundance. Starting with the spinning jenny and Arkwright's spinning frame in the 1760s, the familiar technologies of carding, spinning, and weaving became comprehensively mechanized and harnessed to water power. In England, then in other parts of Britain and in America, factories sprang up that could produce woolen and cotton cloth hundreds of times faster and less expensively than by hand.

No less important to the history of quilting was the related transformation of textile printing technology. The wood block printing of textiles was slow and laborious, because the cloth had to be moved and the block positioned and aligned manually. In 1783 the relatively new technique of copperplate printing was "married" to the technology of water-driven, rotating metal cylinders to create the cylinder printing method for textiles. A single cylinder printing machine could print as much yardage in four minutes as two people with wood blocks could accomplish in six hours.[5] [Plates 16 and 17].

The first wave of the Industrial Revolution came to New England's shores around 1793, when Samuel Slater established his Pawtucket, Rhode Island, mill for spinning cotton. The first power loom to weave cotton fabric appeared in

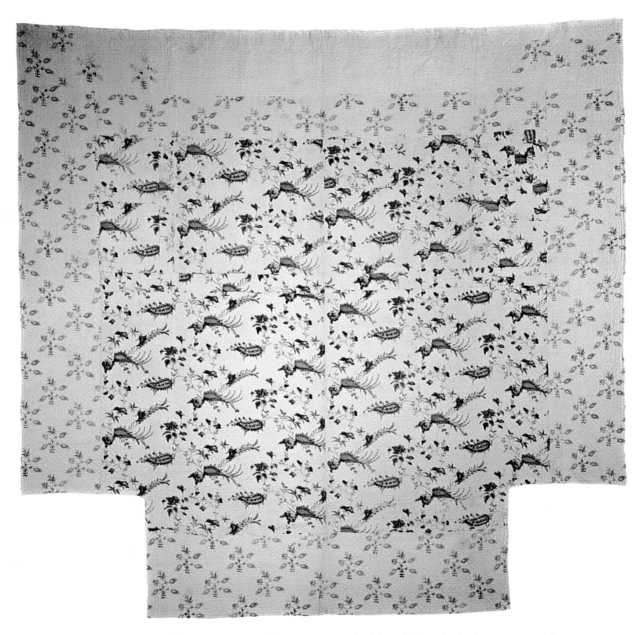

PLATE 18. *Pieced quilt of block-printed and plain linens, c. 1815. The fabric of the quilt's borders was printed by James Copeland Waterman of Massachusetts, whose textile printing blocks are in the collection of the H. F. DuPont Winterthur Museum in Delaware. The maker of this quilt apparently did not have enough of the block-printed fabric to complete her project and attempted to replace it by embroidering copies of the motifs along the top; but she did not finish filling in the empty area, perhaps deciding that it was too much trouble.*

PLATE 19.

Waltham, Massachusetts, in 1814. Textile printing factories were firmly established in New England by the end of the 1820s. By 1840, merchants advertising in the (Worcester) *Massachusetts Spy* could offer domestic calico fabrics as low as four and five cents a yard and fine quality imported calicoes at twenty-five to fifty cents.[6]

PLATE 19. *Whole cloth quilt of copperplate-printed cotton, c. 1790. Apparently, the maker did not care that the fabric was not printed from selvage to selvage; she chose to use the total width of the fabric, leaving a large white strip near the middle of the quilt. The edging of the quilt is a block-printed stripe, meant to be cut and used as a trimming for valances. This feature suggests that the quilt was originally made with matching bed hangings. Copperplate print by Francis Nixon, Phillipsbridge, Surrey, England.*

PLATE 20. *"About Dry Goods," woodcut from* Peter Parley's Method of Teaching Arithmetic to Children *[(Boston: Carter and Hendee, 1834), 50.]*

Not only were textiles—both plain and printed, ordinary and fancy—far cheaper than ever before, they were also more vibrant and colorful, due to innovations in dye technology. The first successful "single" green dye was developed in 1809, making the printing of yellow over blue no longer necessary. This both reduced textile printing costs and substantially improved the accuracy of color registration. A number of new mineral dyes, based on metallic compounds rather than traditional vegetable products, were developed for manufacturing use in the early nineteenth century; they provided sharper, brighter colors on printed textiles such as manganese bronze, chrome yellow, and chrome orange [Plate 21].

As prices fell sharply in the early nineteenth century, New England families had access to an unprecedented supply of fabrics, designs, and colors, and began to be able to own more and better clothing, curtains, and carpets. As a consequence, women could use their cloth more generously, and scraps and extra lengths of fabric were common in most households. Women could also afford to buy "new calico, to cut into various ingenious figures [for]…patchwork."[7] Many of them used this new abundance to expand and improve on the mosaic patchwork tradition, experimenting with pieced designs for bed quilts.

As textiles, including quilts, became increasingly available in New England life, they lost much of their monetary value relative to other goods. The whole cloth quilts of the eighteenth century were worth far more in their own time than the pieced quilts of the early nineteenth century. The probate inventories for Sturbridge, Massachusetts, households from the 1770s to the 1840s reveal a steep decline in the relative value of most quilts. (The first quilt in a Sturbridge inventory appeared in 1772, in the estate of Samuel Freeman, Jr.) When values are adjusted for comparability, the quilts found in eighteenth-century inventories were appraised at over five times the value of those of the 1830s and 1840s ($5.97 vs. $1.13). By the second quarter of the nineteenth century, textiles were no longer the expensive, prestigious items they had been in previous centuries; calico bed quilts had become affordable for the great majority of households.

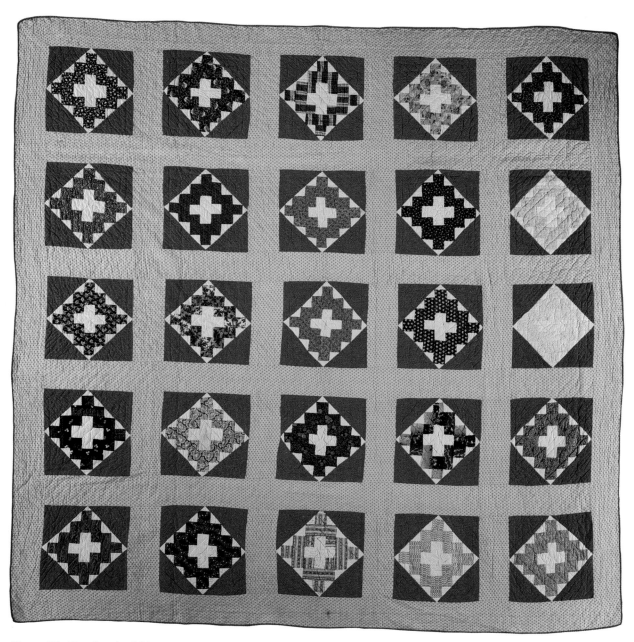

PLATE 21. *Pieced quilt of fabrics woven and printed c. 1840-1850. The quilt itself was made c. 1870 by Emogene Tifft Ward from fabrics produced by John Ward and Sons, textile printers of Riverton, Connecticut. The fabrics in this quilt suggest that the firm, established around 1837, specialized in printing less expensive calicoes, including the chrome orange spotted calico used in the sashing.*

PATCHWORK IS GOOD ECONOMY 39

PLATE 22. *Selection of pieced pockets of printed cottons and linens, eighteenth and early nineteenth centuries. In the eighteenth century, women pieced the relatively few fabric scraps available into useful small items such as potholders, sewing kits called "housewifes," and pockets, such as those seen here. A pocket was worn tied around the waist and was reached through a slit in the side seam of the wearer's skirt. The piecing of these items was simple, usually in squares that made the most use of a scrap with the least amount of effort. Some women continued to make pockets into the early nineteenth century.*

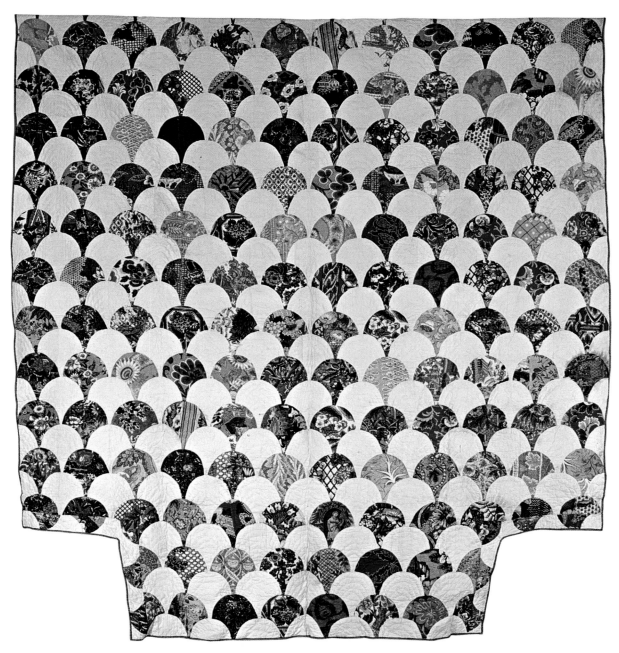

PLATE 23. *Scallop mosaic template-pieced quilt of printed cottons, c. 1820. Many New England bed quilts of the early nineteenth century continued to follow the template-pieced English fashion.*

Quilts Reused and Recycled

New fabrics predominated in many early New England quilts, but there are also numerous examples of the recycling and reuse of fabrics—object lessons in both frugality and sentiment. Several quilts in the collection of Old Sturbridge Village were clearly used to salvage what were valued textiles handed down from a previous generation. One red wool whole cloth quilt is actually made of an eighteenth-century quilted petticoat, whose original elongated rectangular shape has been cut in half and resewn to form a square. The quilt has been made bed-size by the addition of wide strips of red wool along two sides, which have then been quilted to additional batting and backing [Plate 24].

Nancy Newton of Marlborough, New Hampshire, made a quilt that incorporates an eighteenth-century, silk-embroidered pocket at the top of its center panel [Plate 25]. She must have valued the pocket highly, for she went to the trouble of embroidering matching panels for the rest of the quilt's center. She embroidered her name and birth date, 1801, within a heart at the bottom [Plate 26]. The maker of another bed quilt, this one from Hadley, Massachusetts, was concerned to salvage the treasured pieces of what was probably an eighteenth-century set of embroidered bed hangings. She incorporated numerous pieces of this earlier work into her creation, the rest of which is pieced from early nineteenth-century printed textiles [Plate 27].

The patchwork quilt of popular imagination, of course, has always been both frugal and nostalgic—a vehicle for using up a household's scraps of worn-out printed cotton clothing. By the 1820s, there were enough such scraps in New England households for this to be possible. In her 1822 quilt Lucretia Cogswell Rees could draw on what must have been a capacious bag of scraps to create a constellation of calico stars [Plate 28]. Sally Brown of Plymouth, Vermont, wrote in her diary on October 19, 1833, that she "…began to piece a bed quilt out of two old calico gowns." The quilt in Plate 29 is unlikely to have been made by Sally Brown, but a careful look at it indicates that it too has been pieced from the scraps of what were probably two old calico gowns. Some of the large diamonds in its pattern are made of smaller fragments, stitched together to form a piece large enough to cut into the required shape.

PLATE 24. *Wool quilt pieced from an eighteenth-century quilted petticoat, c. 1800-1825.*

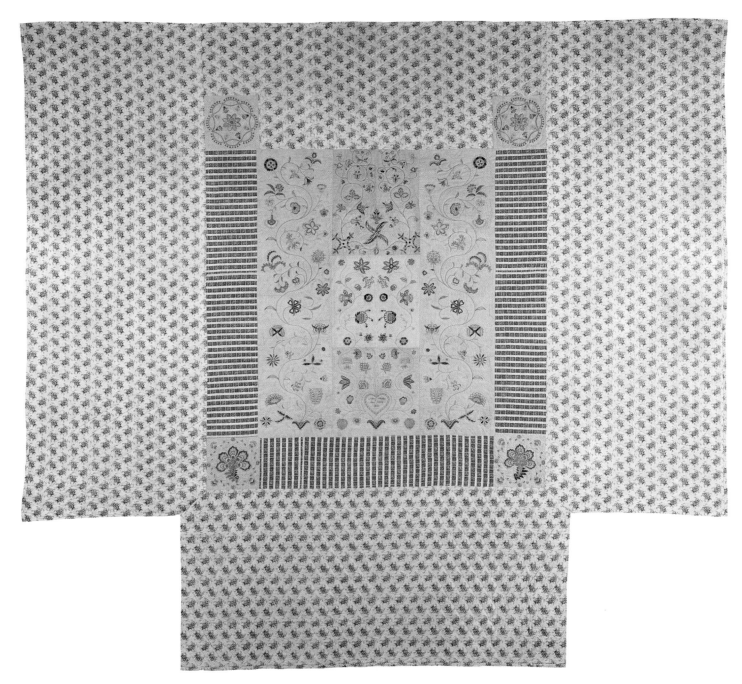

PLATE 25. *Quilt of printed and silk-embroidered cottons incorporating an eighteenth-century embroidered pocket, c. 1825-1850, made by Nancy Newton (1801-1887) of Marlborough, New Hampshire.*

PLATE 26. *(Detail) Quilt of printed and silk-embroidered cottons by Nancy Newton, c. 1825-1850. Here the quilter embroidered her name and birth date and enclosed them in a heart.*

PLATE 27. *Pieced quilt of printed cottons with cotton embroidery, Hadley, Massachusetts, c. 1815-1830. This quilt has been pieced from what was probably a set of earlier bed hangings.*

The Practicality of Quilts

In the same year that Sally Brown noted the reuse of her old calico gowns, Lydia Maria Child wrote in *The American Frugal Housewife*: "...patchwork is good economy....a large family may be kept out of idleness, and a few shillings saved, by thus saving scraps of gowns, curtains, &c."[8] If patchwork saved money, however, it was not because the value of a scrap quilt was less than that of a blanket—quilts were consistently valued higher than blankets in household inventories—but because such a quilt utilized materials already on hand that otherwise had no use. Stitching together a quilt made it unnecessary to purchase another blanket or a bed covering.

Quilts, with their hundreds of stitched chambers that used both batting and trapped air as insulation, were also generally judged to be warmer than blankets. The traveler James Montgomery noted that "...one good [quilt] is certainly superior to a pair of Scotch blankets," and the housekeeping advice writer Eliza Leslie believed that one whole cloth chintz quilt, "...laid *under* the bed-spread" was "...equal in warmth to three heavy blankets...."[9]

Although pieced quilts were, under the conditions of the early nineteenth century, practical and economical in many respects, economy was far from being the sole or even the primary motive of their creators. Attractive and inexpensive calicoes had a powerful allure, and many early calico quilts have a mix of scrap fabrics and materials that have surely been carefully chosen to enhance or finish their design. Sarah Snell Bryant, of Cummington, Massachusetts, noted in 1819 that she "rode to Mr. Mitches store [and] bought some calico for a border to a bed quilt...." Lucretia Cogswell Rees used a wide variety of scrap fabrics to make her star design quilt, but she probably used newly bought cottons as well. A pieced calico quilt made in Fitchburg, Massachusetts, around 1835 is made with fabrics whose limited number and careful arrangement strongly suggest that they were bought for the purpose [Plate 33].

PLATE 28. *Pieced quilt of plain and printed cottons, star variation, c. 1822. This quilt is signed and dated on the reverse by Lucretia Cogswell Rees, who married Isaac Mighles Rees of Stockbridge, Massachusetts, in 1822.*

PLATE 29. *Pieced quilt made of two printed cottons, c. 1830-1840. The alternating light and dark diamonds form the simplest of block designs.*

ENDNOTES

1. Alice Morse Earle, ed., *Diary of Anna Green Winslow, A Boston School Girl of 1771* (Boston and New York: Houghton Mifflin, 1894), 62. The earliest known written reference to patchwork in America can be found in the diary of Anna Green Winslow, when on April 18,1772, she comments that she has exchanged a piece of patchwork for some lace mitts.
2. Quoted in Betty Ring, *Girlhood Embroidery* (New York: A. A. Knopf, 1993), vol. 1, 53.
3. George Francis Dow, *The Arts & Crafts of New England, 1704-1775* (Topsfield, Mass.: The Wayside Press, 1927), 276.
4. Prices were taken from the Account Book of John Butler, Ashford, Conn., 1794–1828, Old Sturbridge Village Research Library.
5. Wendy Hefford, *The Victoria and Albert Museum's Textile Collection, Vol. I, Design for Printed Textiles in England from 1750 to 1850* (London: Victoria & Albert Enterprises, 1992), 14. Block printing by hand remained in use for some fine quality cotton fabrics through the first half of the nineteenth century.
6. See *Massachusetts Spy* (Worcester), 1840, passim.
7. Eliza Leslie, *The House Book: or a Manual of Domestic Economy* (Philadelphia: Carey & Hart, 1843), 311.
8. Lydia Maria Child, *The American Frugal Housewife* (Boston: Carter, Hendee and Babcock, 1833), 1.
9. James Montgomery, *A Practical Detail of the Cotton Manufacture of the United States of America* (Glasgow, 1840), 49; Leslie, *The House Book*, 313.

Chapter III

A Beggar's Patch-Work

Pieced Calico Quilts

Block Piecing

The first half of the nineteenth century was a time of transition and creativity in New England quiltmaking. Whole cloth wool quilts, pieced wool quilts, cut-out chintz appliqué quilts, template-pieced quilts, and pieced-block calico quilts all survive from this period in substantial numbers and are abundantly documented in the historical record. In the earlier years of this period, most New England quilt design was still based on English precedent, which remained influential throughout these years. But many quiltmakers were experimenting with combinations of construction and design techniques, such as joining cut-out chintz work with template piecing or integrating template-pieced mosaic patchwork with pieced-block design.

BY THE LATE 1820s, patchwork quilting was no longer the preserve of the elite.

Susannah Anderson Howard's miniature-pieced quilt is one of the most remarkable of these examples of experimentation with pattern and design [Plate 1]. Her design begins in the long-established English style, with a central medallion of template-pieced hexagon mosaic patchwork. But surrounding the center she has created a sequence of borders, each made up of many different pieced blocks. In their playful geometry, the borders embody the transition in patchwork design from English tradition to the distinctly American pieced-block style, which began to dominate in New England and

PLATE 30. *(Detail) Miniature-pieced quilt of printed cottons, c. 1840. Susannah Anderson Howard of Ware, Massachusetts, used a variety of fabrics for this simple, diamond-in-a-square patchwork design, including an eighteenth-century block print and early nineteenth-century loom-quilted Marseilles vesting, along with cylinder-printed cottons and woven stripe fabrics.*

PLATE 31. *(Detail) Miniature-pieced quilt of printed cottons, c. 1840, Susannah Anderson Howard. In the star blocks of these two borders, the quilter experimented with the different effects that could be achieved using light and dark fabrics.*

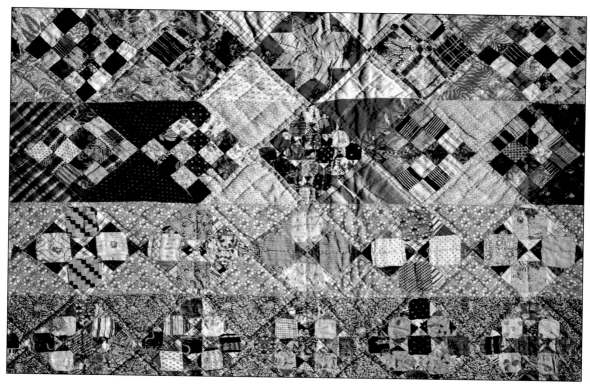

PLATE 32. *(Detail) Miniature-pieced quilt of printed cottons, c. 1840, Susannah Anderson Howard. In these four borders we can see several different four- and nine-patch variations of block piecing.*

elsewhere in the United States in the second quarter of the nineteenth century.

Block patterns typically begin with a square, which is then divided into a symmetrical geometric design by lines that can be either straight or curved. Today, quilters seem able to find virtually infinite variety in these designs, but in the first half of the nineteenth century, quilt blocks were usually designed with simple grid-like divisions of four, nine, or sixteen equal "patches," giving rise to the terms "four-patch" or "nine-patch block." Within the overall pattern, each small square patch could be further subdivided, to be itself built up of smaller triangles, rectangles, or other geometric shapes. In template-pieced mosaic patchwork, a quilter would simply add, piece by piece, to an ever-growing quilt under construction. The maker of a pieced-block quilt would separately assemble as many blocks as she needed, sew the blocks together in strips, and then sew the strips together to complete the quilt top.

Block pattern quilts break with patchwork tradition in another way: in their construction, women abandoned the use of paper templates and sewed the fabric pieces together with a running stitch. While English makers of patchwork occasionally used a running stitch, on the whole they continued to prefer paper template piecing long after Americans had largely abandoned the practice. As late as the 1930s, the British writer of a patchwork and quilting instruction book suggested the use of paper templates, even when constructing American-style block patchwork.[1] By discarding the laborious steps of cutting out hundreds of templates and stitching pieces of fabric onto them, American quilters saved themselves a good deal of time. But in some cases the quality of their work suffered. Without the exacting guidance provided by the templates, patchwork blocks could become irregular, with truncated triangle points and offset corners. The risk of imperfect results did not outweigh the desire of busy American housewives for speed and efficiency.

In constructing their pieced block tops, New England quiltmakers created their own parameters of design. They could sew the blocks together edge-to-edge or insert strips of "sashing" between them. Blocks could be set square, with their sides parallel to the edges of the quilt, or "on point," to form diamond shapes. Pieced blocks might be alternated with "plain" blocks of a single fabric, or two different pieced blocks might be stitched together in another version of an alternating pattern.

Many New England women devoted considerable thought and ingenuity to the design of their pieced-block quilts. Sarah Snell Bryant of Cummington, Massachusetts, drew quilt block designs in her diary in 1808, dividing squares into grids and penciling in alternate patches. One of her sketches illustrated a clever reversal of the usual quilting practice. Pieced blocks were normally bordered with solid sashing; Sarah designed a solid block with pieced sashing instead. In constructing the borders of her miniature-pieced quilt, Susannah Anderson Howard pieced numerous variations of four-patch, five-patch, nine-patch, and sixteen-patch blocks; she also pieced star patterns and a block divided with curved lines, which she probably knew as Orange Peel [Plates 30, 31, and 32].

PLATE 33. *Pieced quilt of printed cottons, nine-patch variation, c. 1835, from Fitchburg, Massachusetts. The maker of this quilt was able to arrange her colors so that the center of the quilt seems almost to glow.*

PLATE 34. *Pieced quilt of printed cottons, nine-patch variation, c. 1845. A clever modification of the usual style of sashing was used to create a zig-zag effect.*

PLATE 35. *Strip-pieced quilt of printed cottons, c. 1835, from the Capen family of Stoughton, Massachusetts. Some fabrics used in this quilt were also used in the other Capen family quilt appearing in Plate 37. Strip piecing, which created a striped effect, was a popular early piecing design, probably English in origin.*

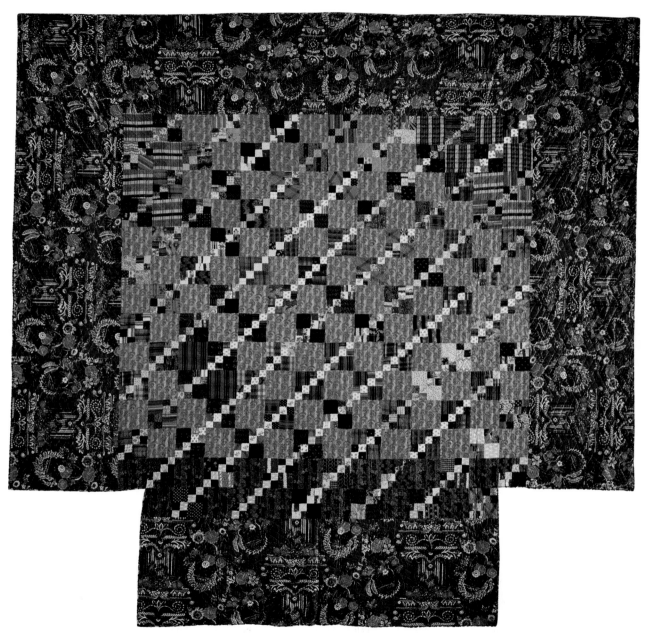

PLATE 36. *Pieced quilt of printed cottons, four-patch variation, c. 1835, from the Wilbur family of Swansea, Massachusetts. Although this quilt has been pieced of scraps, it has a wonderfully graphic quality.*

PLATE 37. *Pieced quilt of printed cottons, nine-patch variation, c. 1835, from the Capen family of Stoughton, Massachusetts. This quilt shares some fabrics with the one in Plate 35. It is another scrap-pieced quilt that achieves a striking design.*

PLATE 38. *Pieced quilt of solid and plain cottons, marked in cross-stitch at center top, "S. S. Larkin 1833." Designed around a circle, this pattern required more complex geometry than the more common four- and nine-patch block designs.*

Naming Quilts

Relatively little is known about the names used for specific patchwork designs in the years before 1850; many names familiar today seem to have been coined in the late nineteenth century or even later. However, certain patterns appear to have been commonly known by name in New England as far back as the eighteenth century. In 1798 Eliza Southgate, who was attending school in Boston, wrote home in dismay about the theft of her quilts: "You mention in your letter about my pieces, which you say you imagine are purloined; I am very sorry if they are, for I set more by them than any of my pieces; one was the Mariner's Compass, and the other was a Geometrical piece."[2] The "Geometrical piece" was undoubtedly a template-pieced mosaic patchwork quilt. The Mariner's Compass pattern is still today a measure of a quilter's skill, with its difficult-to-piece points [Plate 40]. It is no wonder that Eliza was saddened by the loss of her quilts.

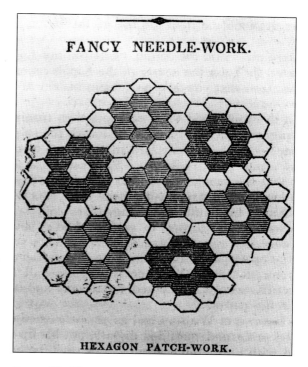

PLATE 39. *Hexagon or Honeycomb pattern for a template-pieced patchwork quilt from* The Lady's Book, *1835.*

In their handwritten weaving drafts (detailed weaving instructions) dating from the 1790s to the 1820s for woven "overshot" coverlets, Peace and Patience Kirby of Dartmouth, Massachusetts, often gave their patterns names such as "blazing star," "wagon wheels," and "Irish beauty." The design they called "orring [orange] Peal" has the same arrangement of curved lines within a square that is seen in the quilt block still called Orange Peel today; it is therefore likely that the Orange Peel block, like the Mariner's Compass, received its name in this early period [Plates 41, 42, and 43].

A patchwork design was named in an American publication as early as 1831.

Eliza Leslie included an illustration and directions for a mosaic patchwork design in *The American Girl's Book*, calling it both "honeycomb" and "hexagon" patchwork. (It is today sometimes known as Grandmother's Flower Garden [Plate 39].) *The Lady's Book* (later *Godey's Lady's Book*), America's influential monthly guide to fashion in dress and decor, reprinted Leslie's description and illustration in 1835. In 1849 a story in *Godey's*, "The Quilting Party," mentioned—as old fashioned and rustic—pieced quilts called "rising star," "Job's trouble," and "Irish chain." [3] The last name has long been used to describe a distinctive style of pieced-block design; the earliest dated pieced quilt in the collection of Old Sturbridge Village is a variation on the Irish Chain pattern, with friendship sentiments and the year "1806" worked into its quilting [Plate 44].

PLATE 40. *(Detail) Pieced quilt of printed cottons, Mariner's Compass design, c. 1840, made by Emily Gordon of Springfield, Massachusetts.*

PLATE 41. *Pieced quilt of printed cottons, Orange Peel design, c. 1835-1840, made by Sophia Young (b. 1794) of Athol, Massachusetts.*

PLATE 41.

A BEGGAR'S PATCH-WORK   63

PLATE 42. *Manuscript "orring Peal" weaving draft, Peace and Patience Kirby, Dartmouth, Massachusetts, c. 1798-1826. Weaving drafts provide shorthand instructions for passing the threads of the warp through the loom's heddles, which are controlled by harnesses. Treadles raise and lower the harnesses, allowing the weaver to throw the shuttle with the weft thread across the warp, thus creating the design. In this early example of a weaving draft, which is for a four-harness overshot design, the warp threads are numbered and organized in groups of three and six, and the harnesses are represented by horizontal lines. [Old Sturbridge Village Research Library]*

PLATE 43. *Reproduction overshot wool and cotton coverlet, "orring Peal" design. This coverlet was woven at Old Sturbridge Village following the Kirby weaving draft in Plate 42. This woven version of the Orange Peel pattern is virtually identical in its geometry to the quilted version in Plate 41.*

PLATE 44. *Pieced quilt of plain and printed cottons, Irish Chain variation, 1806. Quilted with mottoes of "Content Faith Happiness" and "Love and Friendship" within hearts; also "ATE."*

Stenciled Quilts

Some early New England pieced quilts, as well as other bed covers, contain stenciled elements—decorative motifs, even names and dates, that have been painted on the fabric using paints and cut paper patterns. In the last quarter of the eighteenth century, when wallpaper was not yet widely available in the New England countryside, some houses were decorated with stenciled walls and floors. By the 1820s, wallpaper and carpets were far more common than stenciled wall and floor decoration (although the practice had not yet disappeared), but stenciling had become a widely popular technique for decorating on a smaller scale. Using short-bristle brushes called "scrubs," imported pigments, and oiled paper stencils, young New England women studying art at academies or female seminaries created "theorems" on velvet to be framed and hung in their parlors [Plate 46]. Painted tinware and furniture, particularly chairs, went to market with stenciled designs [Plate 45]. Women in thousands of households enthusiastically added stenciled motifs to window shades and curtains, tablecloths, clothing accessories, fire screens—and quilts [Plate 47].

The use of stenciling on quilts is a vernacular decorative technique almost entirely confined to the northeastern United States; only one stenciled quilt has been discovered whose documented history places it south of New Jersey. Early stenciled bed covers are rare; the large quilt collection at Old Sturbridge Village has two stenciled bed quilts [Plates 48 and 50], along with five unquilted bedcovers. Unquilted stenciled bed covers are not pieced. Instead, the stenciled designs have been applied across the fabric, usually, if not always, in an attempt to create a symmetrical design. The great majority of stenciled quilts, however, are pieced. Quilters stenciled their fabrics, cut them into shapes, and combined them with printed cottons to create block-pieced designs.

In the small rural community of Eastford, Connecticut, seventeen-year-old Clarissa Moore created a striking stenciled quilt in 1837. She made it by stenciling many small motifs of flowers, birds, and stars onto white cotton

PLATE 45. *Dressing table of pine or maple painted yellow, made in 1835 by Grover Spooner of Barre, Massachusetts. It has been decorated with stencils, most prominent of which is a fruitbowl design in bronze.*

PLATE 46. *Stencil equipment of Lucy Goodale (1820-1840), who took lessons in this technique while a student at Mount Holyoke Seminary in South Hadley, Massachusetts.*

A BEGGAR'S PATCH-WORK   67

PLATE 47. *Stenciled window curtain, c. 1820-1850.*

fabric and then cutting them into triangular and small square pieces. She then pieced the stenciled fabrics back together, along with several different printed calicoes, to form a design of eight-pointed stars alternating with large chintz diamonds. Clearly proud of her work, she also stenciled her name and the year, and pieced them into the quilt as well [Plates 48 and 49].

It has been suggested that stenciling offered quilters an inexpensive alternative to purchasing hand-block printed fabrics, but this seems very unlikely for the 1820s and 1830s. [5] Elegant and inexpensive cylinder-printed calicoes were widely available by this time, and the imported pigments used for creating stenciled designs were not cheap. Stenciling was, in all probability, simply another way for quilters to add interest and variety to their pieces. It is possible that young Clarissa Moore learned to paint "theorems" with stencils as part of her schooling and simply applied it to her quilting. It is also possible that she learned it in the course of work, since many young women in New England were employed in hand-decorating tinware and chairs.

PLATE 48. *Pieced and stenciled quilt of plain and printed cottons, made in 1837 by Clarissa Moore (1820-1912) of Eastford, Connecticut.*

PLATE 49. *(Detail) Pieced and stenciled quilt by Clarissa Moore.*
The pieced star of printed fabrics is surrounded by the pieced and
stenciled flowers, leaves, and stars, as well as the stenciled "1837"
date repeated four times.

PLATE 50. *Stenciled quilt of plain and printed cottons, c. 1820-1850. The unknown maker of this quilt used large-scale designs that are typical of framed theorems.*

"A Beggar's Patch-work"

By the second quarter of the nineteenth century, patchwork quilting could no longer be considered a "genteel" needle craft, the preserve of the elite. Once most households could afford printed calicoes, it seems that upper-class women began to abandon calico patchwork and to view pieced calico quilts as gauche, ugly, and unfashionable. The women writers of household advice books and domestic fiction expressed the fashionable consensus. Eliza Leslie wrote haughtily in *The House Book* in 1843: "Patch-work quilts of old calico are only seen in inferior chambers; but they are well worth making for servants' beds. The custom of buying new calico, to cut into various ingenious figures, for what was called handsome patch-work, has become obsolete." [6]

In her story "The Patch-Work Quilt," published in 1846, Catharine Maria Sedgwick described a hexagon-pieced calico quilt as "a beggar's patch-work." [7] Writing some years later, the author of *The Lady's Manual of Fancy-Work* of 1858 was even harsher: "Of the patchwork with calico, I have nothing to say. Valueless indeed must be the time of that person who can find no better use for it than to make ugly counterpanes and quilts of pieces of cotton. Emphatically is the proverb true of cotton patchwork, *Le jeu ne vaut pas la chandelle!* It is not worth either candle or gas light." [8]

New England's own Lydia Maria Child took a more temperate view of calico patchwork but still dismissed it as suitable only for families that needed to pinch pennies or entertain small children. She wrote in *The American Frugal Housewife* in 1832: "It is indeed a foolish waste of time to tear cloth into bits for the sake of arranging it anew in fantastic figures; but a large family may be kept out of idleness, and a few shillings saved, by thus using scraps of gowns, curtains, &c." [9] Writing two years later, Child dismissed patchwork as "old fashioned" but allowed that it was useful for keeping children busy. [10]

Godey's Lady's Book was essentially in agreement. When the magazine reprinted the Hexagon patchwork pattern, it was to recommend it for children. When *Godey's* subsequently published quilt patterns, they were almost always for traditional English mosaic designs, and readers were urged to make

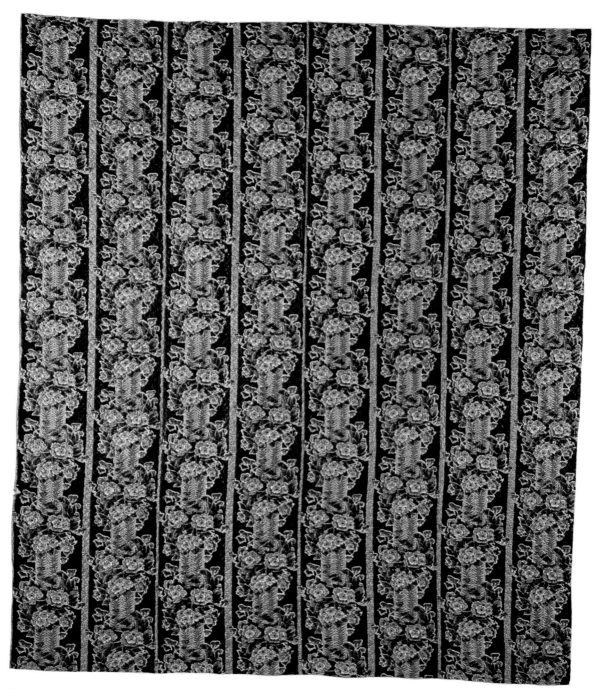

PLATE 51. *Whole cloth chintz quilt, pillar print, c. 1830.*

them out of expensive—and genteel—silks and velvets rather than printed cottons.

After disparaging calico patchwork, Eliza Leslie wrote confidently in 1843 that "Quilts are now made entirely of the same sort of dark calico or furniture chintz." But the large number of surviving calico patchwork quilts from the 1840s, 1850s, and beyond, as well as the continuing diversity of quilt designs, make it clear that most New England quilters were paying her little heed. It is true that some New England women were returning to whole cloth quilting in chintz, but very often they did not use the dark and subdued fabrics that Miss Leslie preferred. Many New England whole cloth chintz quilts made after 1825 indicate a continuing propensity for bright colors and lively images; they are made from colorful and flamboyant prints, with large-scale designs of pillars, flowers, and birds [Plate 51].

Patchwork Quilts and Popular Taste

When describing New England in 1840, the Scottish visitor James Montgomery clearly linked calico quilts with "country people." With their varied colors, pieced designs, and figured calico prints, early nineteenth-century patchwork quilts fit far more comfortably into the decorative schemes of ordinary rural households than elite urban ones. In the years after 1800, many thousands of New England families—artisans, country merchants and professionals, and middling farmers—were moving out of the comparative material austerity of the eighteenth century. They began to use more paint and wallpaper as they became increasingly affordable, to purchase inexpensive mass-produced chairs and other furniture, to use mass-produced, often transfer-printed, ceramics in great quantity, and to put carpets on the floors and curtains on the windows. [11]

Houses in the countryside often displayed exuberant combinations of color and pattern, in sharp contrast to the more restrained practice of prosperous city households. This is attested by a careful study of the Emerson Bixby House, a well-preserved country blacksmith's house built in Barre, Massachusetts, around

1807 and relocated to Old Sturbridge Village in 1986. Around 1815, the Bixby House had a truly eye-popping interior decorative scheme. At that time, the "best room" of the house had its doors, wainscoting, chair rail, and chimney breast painted Prussian blue. The floor was painted red, the baseboard around the room's perimeter was brown, and the mantelpiece was both red and brown. Above the chair rail, the walls were covered with a printed wallpaper of white, pink, and green-on-blue. [12]

The chairs that went into such lively interiors were often painted yellow or green, and were stenciled; other pieces of furniture might be painted with faux graining. Accompanying them were colorful printed cotton bed hangings, tinware containers painted with bright red and green floral patterns, and transfer-printed English ceramics in blue and green mixed with green- and yellow-banded mocha ware and other hand-decorated pieces. In their range of contrasting colors and prints, and their diverse designs, patchwork quilts echoed and amplified this exuberance. This popular rural aesthetic was not prized by those who made pronouncements about fashionable styles in quilting.

Comforters

The comforter, or "comfortable," was a variation on the whole cloth chintz or calico quilt that first appeared in New England—based on references in women's diaries and probate inventories—in the 1820s. A comforter had the same three-layered structure as a quilt, consisting of a face fabric, batting, and backing, but it was not continuously stitched together. Instead, the face and backing were attached at intervals with a single stitch of thread or yarn that was tied off and clipped. Sometimes comforters were equated with whole cloth quilts by less knowledgeable observers, but quilt-making New England diarists clearly distinguished between the two and always wrote that they had "tied comforters," never that they had tied a quilt.

Probate inventories registered the difference, valuing comforters generally lower than quilts but higher than blankets. Similar in appearance to whole cloth quilts, providing the same warmth, but much quicker to make, comforters offered

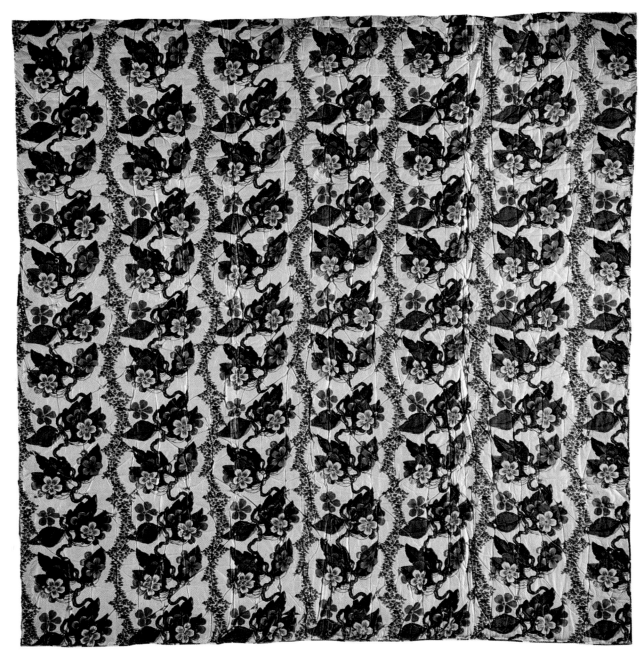

PLATE 52. *Tied chintz comforter, c. 1830-1840.*

PLATE 53. *Whole cloth chintz quilt, c. 1850. The printed design of the fabric simulates patchwork.*

PLATE 54. *Woman's chintz jacket, c. 1850-1870. This fabric also has been printed to simulate patchwork.*

an efficient and fashionable alternative to quilts. However, it is clear, both from surviving examples and from written documents, that New England women preferred bed quilts of calico patchwork.

Imitation Patchwork

When it came to pieced calico quilts, British and possibly American textile manufacturers paid no more heed to fashion's decrees than did New England quilters themselves. Earlier in the century, they had recognized the popularity of cut-out chintz appliqué quilts and had begun to print designs especially for use by women working in that style. By the 1840s, textile printers, recognizing the continuing popularity of pieced calico quilts, began to print cotton fabrics with designs that simulated patchwork. The whole cloth quilt shown in Plate 53 is a remarkably ironic document in the history of fashion. It is made of just the sort of dark chintz that the most genteel taste had decreed for quilts, yet it appears to be pieced from old calicoes!

ENDNOTES

1. Agnes M. Miall, *Patchwork Old and New* (London: The Woman's Magazine Office, 1937), 65.
2. Clarence Cook, ed., *A Girl's Life Eighty Years Ago: Selections from the Letters of Eliza Southgate Bowne* (New York: Charles Scribner's Sons, 1887), 15.
3. T. S. Arthur, "The Quilting Party," *Godey's Lady's Book*, 39, no. 4 (September 1849): 185-6.
4. Diana Church, "The Baylis Stenciled Quilt," *Uncoverings…1983…Research Papers of the American Quilt Study Group*, 4 (Mill Valley, Calif., 1984), 75-86.
5. This is suggested in Patsy and Myron Orlofsky, *Quilts in America* (New York: Abbeville Press, 1974), 187. It is highly unlikely that practitioners of stenciling used "garden fruits and vegetables" for their pigments, as is suggested in Church, p. 76.
6. Eliza Leslie, *The House Book: or, A Manual of Domestic Economy* (Philadelphia: Carey & Hart, 1843), 311.
7. Catharine Maria Sedgwick, "The Patch-Work Quilt," *The Columbian Lady's and Gentleman's Magazine*, 5 (March 1846). Reprinted in Cuesta Ray Benberry and Carol Pinney Crabb, *A Patchwork of Pieces: An Anthology of Early Quilt Stories, 1845-1940* (Paducah, Ky.: American Quilter's Society, 1993), 24-33.
8. Mrs. Pullan, *The Lady's Manual of Fancy-Work* (New York: Dick & Fitzgerald, 1858), 95.
9. Lydia Maria Child, *The American Frugal Housewife* (Boston: Carter, Hendee and Babcock, 1833), 1.
10. Child, *The Little Girl's Own Book* (Boston: Carter, Hendee and Babcock, 1832), 225.
11. Jack Larkin, *The Reshaping of Everyday Life, 1790-1840* (New York: Harper Collins, 1988), 121-148.
12. Myron Stachiw, "The Color of Change: A Nineteenth-Century Massachusetts House," in Roger W. Moss, ed., *Paint in America, The Colors of Historic Buildings* (Washington, D.C.: National Trust for Historic Preservation, 1994), 128-137.

Chapter IV

More Beautiful Than Any Other

Fashionable Quilts in the Second Quarter of the Nineteenth Century

Marseilles, Mersailles, Marcella, Marcels, Marseils, Marsells

In July of 1802, Sarah Snell Bryant wrote a terse diary entry, "finished a jacket for the Dr., Marsells quilt." She almost certainly meant that she had made her physician husband a jacket of purchased Marseilles quilting—a fabric that was not quilted by hand but produced on a specialized loom. The process that accomplished this was patented in England in 1762-1763 by George Glasgow and Robert Elder. Using the centuries-old draw loom, which manipulated warp threads by individually controlled heddles, it was capable of "weaving together two, three, and four pieces of single cloth, so that they will appear as if stitched together." Fabrics "in imitation of the common manner of quilting," could be produced, the inventors asserted, "as of India, French and Marseilles quilting." [1]

WHITEWORK QUILTS reflected the "high" urban version of the Neoclassical style.

Since the seventeenth century, textile workers in Provence had produced intricately quilted, corded, and stuffed whole cloth bed quilts, petticoats, waistcoats, and yardage, and exported them through the port of Marseilles. Such work had a long history in that region of France, dating back to the medieval period. Many motifs and designs common to eighteenth-century English, and subsequently American, quilting may actually have been derived from this early French quilting—which in its turn, had been influenced by medieval and Renaissance Italian needlework. [2]

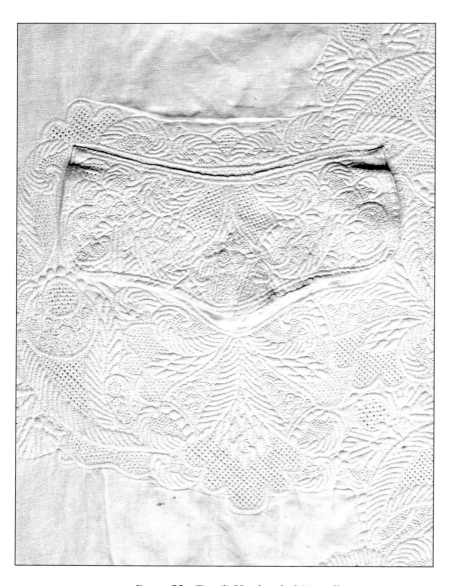

PLATE 55. *(Detail) Hand-quilted Marseilles waistcoat, c. 1770-1800, English or French, with elaborate quilting around the pocket.*

What New Englanders recognized as Marseilles quilting consisted of designs worked on solid-colored silk, linen, and, later, cotton. In the eighteenth century it was characterized by great elaboration, with channeled rows of cording worked in spirals and waves, or in exotic foliate, animal, and figural motifs, often organized around a central medallion. Sometimes individual elements received extra stuffing to give them even more dimension. This quilting style was taught as a fashionable needlework technique to young ladies by private instructors or in New England academies. Eleanor Druitt had advertised in 1771 in the *Boston News-Letter* that she taught "French Quilting." English quilters also imitated the Marseilles style, so that it is difficult, if not impossible, to differentiate between English and French examples.

PLATE 56. *Loom-quilted Marseilles bed cover, c. 1825-1850.*

It is likely that both hand-quilted and loom-quilted Marseilles work was imported to America in the last quarter of the eighteenth century; however, period documents and surviving examples suggest that the loom-quilted product dominated the market. In 1787, when Mary Vial Holyoke of Salem, Massachusetts, took a morning shopping trip and "Bought [a] Marseilles Quilt," it was almost certainly of the loom-quilted variety. [3]

Merchants' advertisements often list Marseilles quilting (in a striking variety of spellings) among the materials available for making waistcoats and vests. John Foot and Co. of Tolland, Connecticut, advertised in the *Connecticut Courant* in 1798, "Fresh European & English Goods," including "…a variety of fashionable Mersailles and muslinet Vesting."[4] Another advertisement by Hartford merchants in the *Courant* in 1795 suggests that the popularity of Marseilles quilting may have led English manufacturers to print fabrics in imitation. Among the "Spring Goods rec'd by Ship Ohio from London," it noted that there were "Velvet Vest Shapes" and "Printed Quilting for d[itt]o."[5] Although no fabric printed to resemble Marseilles quilting is known to survive, it seems likely that this is what the advertisement described.

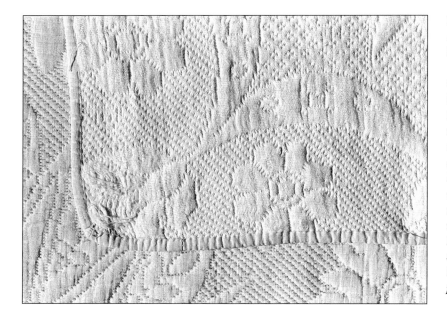

PLATE 57. *(Detail) Loom-quilted Marseilles bed cover, c. 1825-1850. From the back, the worn corner of this bed cover shows the loosely spun cotton roving that forms the inner layer in a loom-quilted Marseilles fabric. Note also that there are no stitches passing through the layers, as with hand quilting. Instead, warp threads are passed through the layers to form the pattern.*

By the early nineteenth century, loom-quilted Marseilles bed covers were made exclusively of white cotton. Their designs were greatly simplified, bearing little resemblance to the intricate figures of the seventeenth and eighteenth centuries, although the central medallion often continued to be the focus of the design. This change was in keeping with the simplified lines and lighter color palette of the Neoclassical style in dress and furniture in Europe and America, a vogue that was initiated by the eighteenth-century excavations of ancient Roman sites, including Pompeii. In New England this fashion came earliest to, and was most faithfully followed in, Boston and other seaports and commercial towns.

In the second quarter of the nineteenth century, loom-quilted Marseilles bed covers became increasingly popular in both urban and rural households influenced by high-style Neoclassical taste, combining elegance with economy. Prices for Marseilles bed quilts and cradle quilts, as well as vests and yardage, fell significantly when the Jacquard mechanism was adapted for use in loom quilting. Because this remarkable machine manipulated warp threads by heddles controlled by punched cards, it greatly speeded up the weaving process and eliminated the need for a second person to assist, as in draw loom weaving.

"More Beautiful Than Any Other"

Unlike pieced calico quilts, the widespread availability of loom-quilted Marseilles bed covers did not render them unfashionable. They remained stylish for many years—a longevity that was also reflected in the fashion for a closely related but intricately hand-crafted variety of Marseilles quilt. This was the "whitework" style of hand-stitched white cotton bed quilts, whose popularity extended from the first decade of the nineteenth century through the 1860s. Whitework quilts were subtle and often elegant creations that depended for their effect entirely upon the intricacy of the quilting design and stitching, rather than a combination of color and pattern. They were demanding to create, often incorporating elements of stuffing and cording to enhance the design, and

PLATE 58. *Whitework quilt, c. 1841. Made by Mrs. D. Baker of New Bedford, Massachusetts.*

so they were much admired. Bradford (Vermont) Academy student Augusta Merrill noted enviously in her diary in 1848 that the "…first class girls…have white bed quilts and various other privileges…."[6]

Stuffed and corded dressing table covers of white cotton were another remarkable handmade quilted item emerging out of the fashion for Marseilles bed covers. Like whitework bed quilts, whitework dressing table covers incorporated Neoclassical motifs of cornucopias, swags, grape clusters, and baskets of flowers. These covers often were made in a half-circular shape to fit over a fashionable "demilune" dressing table. An attached ruffled skirt often hid the fact that the table was rough and unfinished, nothing more than a form meant to be covered. Rectangular stuffed and corded covers without skirts, but perhaps with some netted trim around the edges, made an elegant cover for the top of a chest of drawers.

One remarkable surviving whitework quilt, stitched by Mrs. D. Baker (probably Nancy Cheever Baker) of the thriving and relatively cosmopolitan whaling port of New Bedford, Massachusetts, is still accompanied by its silver medal. Mrs. Baker received the award for her quilt in 1841 at the Massachusetts Charitable Mechanic Association Exhibition in Boston, where it was judged to be "More beautiful than *any* other in the Exhibition."[7] Its masterful design centers on an oval frame filled with floral and foliate motifs. An inner border of undulating feathers is

PLATE 59. *Silver medal won by Mrs. D. Baker for her whitework quilt, judged to be "More beautiful than* any *other in the Exhibition" at the Massachusetts Charitable Mechanic Association Exhibition in Boston in 1841.*

cleverly designed so that there is no awkward overlapping at the corners, as seen in the less expertly made calamanco quilt pictured in Plate 7; an outer border of grapevines has received similar attention, so that a leaf falls perfectly in each corner. The background of the design is stitched in closely spaced diagonal lines. It is not known if Mrs. Baker designed the quilt herself, but her execution of the design is similarly perfect, with a highly consistent nine quilting stitches to the inch.

Mrs. Baker's quilt was described in the exhibition guide as "A Quilted Counterpane, in imitation of Marseilles," which both points to the inspiration for this quilt style and clarifies the use of the term "Marseilles" in the first half of the nineteenth century. Consistently, "Marseilles" was used to describe the loom-quilted product, while "white quilt" or "white quilted counterpane" were the names given the hand-stitched version. It is striking that whitework quilts were valued at significantly higher sums than other quilts. A "white counterpane," almost certainly a whitework quilt, in the estate inventory of Francis Wheelock of Sturbridge in 1833 is listed at the substantial value of five dollars, when calico quilts were generally valued at around one dollar.

This disparity in the value and prestige of pieced calico and whitework quilts reflects their opposition in nineteenth-century fashion. Patchwork quilts, as we have noted, were all of a piece with the enthusiastic combination of color and pattern seen in the furnishing of most New England country households—what we might call a rustic or rural vernacular version of the Neoclassical style. Handmade whitework quilts, along with Marseilles bed covers, reflected the "high" urban version of the Neoclassical, with its considerably more subdued palette of colors and much greater concern with simplicity of line. Of course, this was not a completely precise demarcation; patchwork quilts could undoubtedly be found in some humbler city dwellings, there were whitework quilts on the beds of some sophisticated rural households, and at least one remarkable rural quilter, Susannah Anderson Howard, actually worked in both styles [Plates 1 and 2]. But the divide between calico and whitework was real, an aspect of the cultural opposition of country and city in nineteenth-century America. [8]

Red and Green Appliqué Quilts

Beginning in the 1840s, American quiltmaking took another distinctive turn and New Englanders followed. Many quilters began to work with solid or printed red and green cottons in stylized symmetrical foliate and floral designs, which were cut out with the aid of folded paper patterns and appliquéd in repeating blocks onto backgrounds of plain white cotton. The fashion began in Maryland and Pennsylvania, areas heavily influenced by the German design tradition. The emergence of inexpensive and vibrant red and green cotton fabrics in the 1820s and 1830s propelled the style's popularity.

Striking among the many surviving red and green appliqué New England quilts is a lovely example from Braintree, Massachusetts, whose design is based on a large stylized floral bouquet overflowing out of a small urn. The bouquet is enhanced by "twigs" with red berries that are stuffed so that they are round and hard, and small red birds with black silk wings and beaks. The bouquet and urn design is repeated in four blocks, which are surrounded by a border of flowers and berries that flow horizontally from tiny urns [Plate 60].

By the mid-nineteenth century, pieced-block quilts were being influenced by the red, green, and white color scheme of these appliquéd quilts, which continued their popularity through the 1860s. Red and white combinations for pieced-block quilts were particularly popular. Sarah A. Fitch of Norwalk, Connecticut, worked her design of eight-pointed stars within "feathered" squares in just such a bold and attractive combination of colors and fabrics [Plate 61]. Many mid-nineteenth-century quilts combined block patchwork with the appliqué technique, also using the favored red and green fabrics on a white background.

Although these appliquéd quilts were made of inexpensive cotton fabrics, they appear never to have been criticized in the literature of fashion and domestic advice. One reason was undoubtedly the level of skill involved; creating the often complex appliquéd designs could be quite difficult.[9] Another may have been social class; these quilts were mostly the products of women from at least moderately prosperous households, and they did not incorporate scraps or recycled fabrics into their carefully planned designs.

PLATE 60. *Appliqué quilt of red, green, and white cottons, bouquet and urn design, c. 1850, Braintree, Massachusetts. The leaves were originally a uniform green, but those in one corner have changed color to blue over the years, as a flaw in the dye has allowed the yellow pigment to disappear.*

PLATE 61.
*Block-pieced
quilt of plain
white and
printed red
cotton, c. 1840-
1850,
attributed to
Sarah A. Fitch
(1800-1869)
of Norwalk,
Connecticut.*

ENDNOTES

1. B. Woodcroft, ed., *Patents for Inventions: Abridgements of Specifications Relating to Weaving* (London: The Great Seal Patent Office, 1861), 8-9. Quoted in Sally Garoutte, "Marseilles Quilts and their Woven Offspring," *Uncoverings…1982…Research Papers of the American Quilt Study Group*, vol. 3 (Mill Valley, Calif., 1983), 119.

2. Kathryn Berenson, *Quilts of Provence, The Art and Craft of French Quiltmaking* (New York: Henry Holt and Company, 1996), 123.

3. George Francis Dow, ed., *The Holyoke Diaries, 1709-1856* (Salem, Mass.: The Essex Institute, 1911), 118.

4. *Connecticut Courant* (Hartford), July 2, 1798.

5. *Connecticut Courant* (Hartford), May 11, 1795.

6. Diary of Augusta Merrill, 1848-49, Vermont Historical Society. Quoted in Lynn Bonfield, "Diaries of New England Quilters Before 1860," *Uncoverings…1988…Research Papers of the American Quilt Study Group*, vol. 9 (San Francisco, 1989), 188.

7. Massachusetts Charitable Mechanic Association…*Third Exhibition for the Encouragement of Manufactures and the Mechanic Arts*…(Boston, 1841). Pamphlet, American Antiquarian Society, Worcester, Mass.

8. Richard Bushman, *The Refinement of America, Persons, Houses, Cities* (New York: Vintage Books, 1993), 354.

9. New England appliqué quilts could be impressive, but never reached the extraordinary heights of skill exemplified in the Baltimore album quilt—a highly elaborate and technically challenging style in which each appliqué block featured a different design, often including architectural, human, animal, and floral motifs.

Chapter V

Went To A Quilting

Quilting and Sociability

"Finished quilting my bedquilt this forenoon." So wrote Mary Avery White of Boylston, Massachusetts, in her diary on January 26, 1839, understandably satisfied with the completion of her task. In less than two days, she had renewed the usefulness of a worn-out quilt by covering it with new calico and re-stitching the entire surface to anchor the layers together.

Mary White's simple notation reveals the remarkable speed of which a practiced quilter was capable. It was a bitterly cold but bright winter day, so that she could see her stitches, and she worked alone, which was typical of quilters in the cold winter months. However, the significance of her labor becomes most apparent when we look comprehensively at the thirty-two diaries, with nearly 450 separate entries, in which early New England quilt makers tell us about their work. Taken together, these sources reveal a consistent overall pattern across the years and the seasons. [1]

"I WANT YOUR HELP extremely, it is a dull business for me alone."

For the generations of women who labored before the invention of the sewing machine, quilting, whether of bed quilts, petticoats, or quilted cloaks, was a time-consuming process. In the rural New England tradition of "changing works" and "mutual assistance," quilters more often than not were able to work alongside friends and relatives in the neighborhood. In just over half of the diary entries, women recorded assistance from outside the quilter's household for the

PLATE 62. *In the Salem Towne House at Old Sturbridge Village, women re-enact a quilting party of the 1830s.*

completion of all types of quilting projects. "I have a quilt or two to piece and quilt," wrote Elizabeth Huntington in 1802 to Elizabeth Porter Phelps (both of Hadley, Massachusetts) "and I want your help extremely, it is a dull business for me alone."[2] Any time that a few women gathered together to stitch, they enjoyed the opportunity to converse and exchange neighborhood gossip. "In the afternoon Susan Ayer and myself went down to assist Susan Gale in quilting. We had a fine frolic...," Sarah Connell (soon to become Sarah Ayer) noted in her diary in 1809. Indeed, the importance of these gatherings, like other meetings for cooperative work, went far beyond the need to complete a bed quilt or petticoat. Cooperative quilting strengthened bonds between neighbors and offered companionship to the lonely. The forlorn, and haphazardly spelled, 1788 diary entry of spinster Rebecca Dickinson of Hatfield, Massachusetts, underscores the significance of these social interactions in the lives of women: "...yersterday was at brother bilings quilted of a Pink Silk Quilt [petticoat] for Polly church there was Lindy murry there Eunis White in the afternoon come the wife of joseph Dickinson the wife of Rufus Smith tha both quilted in the Silk quilt how lonesome to Come to this old hous after So much Company...."

PLATE 63. *This oak leaf quilting pattern was cut from the program of an 1831 anti-slavery meeting. A quilted petticoat made with this pattern is also in the Old Sturbridge Village collections.*

Neighbors were sometimes called upon for assistance with quilting tasks other than stitching. "Mrs. Wilder spun me some worsted to quilt with," Pamela Brown of Plymouth, Vermont, gratefully acknowledged in 1837. Basting a quilt into the quilting frame was also most easily done with help: "Tuesday Mrs. Hitchcock & I put on her red & blue bed quilt," Elizabeth Porter Phelps noted in 1797. Once the layers of fabric and batting were firmly attached to the frame, a neighbor with artistic talent might be called upon for the greater challenge of drawing an appealing and symmetrical quilting design. Sarah Snell Bryant of Cummington, Massachusetts, was one such nearby artist; she noted on a December afternoon in 1822 that she had gone "to Mr. Briggses to draw a feather on a bedquilt." The cooperative exchange of quilting labor with the Briggs family had persisted for at least twenty years, for in 1802 Sarah had noted that Mrs. Briggs helped her to finish quilting a bed quilt.

In addition to an informal, conversation-filled afternoon of stitching with a few neighbors and the exchange of labor for spinning or drawing a quilting pattern, cooperation in quilting came in the form of a larger work party usually called a "quilting" or "quilting party."[3] These quiltings virtually always included refreshments, often a late afternoon "tea"—a substantial repast in New England. Quiltings often drew large numbers of women. In 1800 Ruth Henshaw Bascom of Leicester, Massachusetts, noted two quilting parties given by her family: thirteen neighborhood friends came to one, while the other was attended by "19 young ladies."

In his remarkable reminiscence of life in rural Enfield, Massachusetts, Francis Underwood described a September quilting around 1840 and the preparations that preceded it:

> Laying out the plan, and sewing together the pieces, occupied women and children in odd hours for months. When the patchwork was completed, it was laid upon the desired lining, with sheets of wadding between, and the combined edges were basted. Long bars of wood—the 'quiltin' frame'—were placed at the four sides; the quilt was attached to the bars by stout thread, and the bars were fastened at the corners with listing [strips of cloth]; then the whole was raised upon the backs of chairs, one at each corner, to serve as trestles.

PLATE 64. *Quilting pattern made of tin, first half of the nineteenth century. This tin shape was sprinkled with chalk or powdered "lead" (graphite) and impressed on the fabric to leave a pattern that quilters could follow.*

Around the quilt, so stretched out at a convenient height, a dozen (more or less) might be at work, seated at the four sides, all following in their stitching the pattern laid down. A more favorable arrangement for a social afternoon could hardly be imagined. The work demanded no thought on the part of those who were familiar with it; and the women, all facing inward as at a square table, and all in best gowns, cambric collars, and lace caps, could gossip to their hearts' content. [4]

Surviving quilting frames from the eighteenth and early nineteenth centuries tell us about the scale and arrangement of quilting parties. Frames with four equal sides, like the one Underwood describes, could accommodate the largest number of quilters. With each side measuring nine or ten feet long, such frames could easily accommodate a dozen quilters and at times must have been used for even larger groups, as diarists sometimes describe quiltings with fifteen or nineteen participants.

This would have made for crowded rooms. "The quilting frame so nearly filled the sitting-room," Underwood recalled, "that there was little space behind the chairs." [5] For women with smaller homes, free-standing quilting frames with only two long sides were probably more suitable. Six quilters might comfortably work with such an arrangement.

Quilts, too, sometimes reveal themselves as the work of many hands. Not all the women invited to quilting parties were excellent quilters; many were surely valued far more as friends and neighbors. Thus, a variety of stitching styles and levels of skill may be found within a single quilt. An early nineteenth-century whole cloth quilt of deep purple wool provides a striking example: on one side, the quilting is delicate and even, with a remarkable twelve stitches to the inch, while on the other side, the stitches are larger and more irregularly spaced— perhaps the work of an inexperienced girl or an older matron whose close vision was poor.

"The Patchwork Quilt," an essay that appeared in *The Lowell Offering* in 1845, suggests that even very young siblings might participate in a quilting party. The author described how a young brother was recruited for "rolling up the quilt as it was finished, snapping the chalk-line, passing thread; wax and scissors," but that he "was determined to assist.... He must take the thread and needle." His sister and her friends "gave him white thread, and appointed him to a very dark piece of calico, so that we might pick it out the easier; but there! to spite us, he did it so nicely that it still remains, a memento of his skill with the needle...." [6]

Good things to eat were normally part of quiltings. The day before a large quilting party was to be held at her home in Hallowell, Maine, in 1791, Martha Moore Ballard baked pies and cakes while her daughter and niece prepared the quilt. Francis Underwood fondly recalled the lavish spread of delectables that might be offered:

> The tea, pale in color, but really strong, was served in delicate old china, with flesh-colored figures; and the fragrance of so many cups filled the room.
> There was bread and butter, hot biscuits..., waffles, peach preserves, apple-and-quince sauce, doughnuts, mince-pie, custard pie, fruit-cake, sponge-cake, and mellow sage cheese. The tablecloth was like satiny snow. Everything was best and daintiest. [7]

The most elaborate quilting parties, usually confined to young people, extended into the evening hours, when gentlemen were invited to join the ladies for a meal and dancing once the quilt was finished. Martha Moore Ballard described a pleasant evening thus passed in 1790: "My girls had some neighbors to help them quilt a bed quilt, 15 ladies. They began to quilt at 3 hour p.m. Finisht and took it out at 7 evening. There were 12 gentlemen took tea. They danced a little while after supper. Behaved exceeding cleverly... were all returned home before the 11th hour." From a young woman's perspective, these quiltings were boisterous fun. Candace Roberts of Bristol, Connecticut, age twenty, recounted her enjoyment of a quilting in 1805: "Went to a quilting at Capt Manross's had a most delightful afternoon, in the evening was very highly entertained with all kinds of company and most excellent music returned home very late."

The merriment of such quilting parties encouraged flirtation and courtship, as in fact they were designed to do. In his memoir of rural Connecticut, Samuel

Goodrich described quiltings as "a real festival, not unfrequently getting young people into entanglements which matrimony alone could unravel."[8] New England diaries do not provide extensive descriptions of the flirtatious games that gave young men and women the opportunity to pair off, but "The Quilting Party," a story published in *Godey's Lady's Book* in 1849, describes just such an occasion. In it, a young male narrator anticipates receiving a kiss from the hostess during the course of a parlor game:

> Soon it became Amy's place to take the floor. She must 'kiss the one she loved best.' What a moment of suspence! Stealthily her eyes wandered around the room; and then her long, dark lashes lay quivering on her beautiful cheeks.
>
> 'Kiss the one you love best,' was repeated by the holder of the pawns.
>
> The fringed lids were again raised.... Our name at last came, in an undertone, from her smiling lips. What a happy moment! The envied kiss was ours....[9]

At the opposite end of the spectrum from parties that ended with courtship and dancing were the quiltings organized by church sewing circles, charitable organizations, and other women's voluntary associations that were just emerging in the early nineteenth century. Often called Female Fragment Societies after the Scripture "gather up the fragments," with which every New England quilter was familiar, these groups were social innovations, mobilizing women to provide for the community's poor, refurbish the meetinghouse, support missionaries, or promote moral reforms. With a battalion of workers, sewing circles could accomplish a great deal in an afternoon. Mary White noted with pride in 1841 that in the Boylston, Massachusetts, sewing circle "nearly 50 Ladies had two cradle quilts & a bed quilt quilted," and in 1843, when thirty ladies of the sewing circle met, "the Females quilted a large bedquilt beside knitting & other sewing...."

These quilts went directly to poor families along with other textiles, or might be sold to raise cash. Quiltings could also be organized to advance very specific, even controversial, social agendas. Mary White was not only an active member of her church's sewing circle, but also the founder of Boylston's Female Antislavery Society; in 1839, she wrote that her daughter "Caroline & myself assisted in quilting the bed quilt at the Hall for the Antislavery cause." Quilts such as the one that Mary helped to make were sold as fund-raisers at Anti-Slavery Fairs. In her review for *The Liberator* of an Anti-Slavery Fair held in Boston in 1837, Lydia Maria Child described a cradle quilt, which "was made of patch-work in small stars; and on the central star was written with indelible ink:

> 'Mother' when around your child
> You clasp your arms in love,
> And when with grateful joy you raise
> Your eyes to God above-
> Think of the negro-mother,
> When her child is torn away-
> Sold for a little slave-oh, then,
> For that poor mother pray!"[10]

Remarkably, this quilt survives in the collection of the Society for the Preservation of New England Antiquities.

Learning to Quilt

The first generation of New England quilters may well have learned from the careful study of English examples or direct instruction by emigrant English seamstresses. But quilting became a widespread skill, learned by young girls as part of their training in the domestic arts. Mothers surely taught their daughters, just as they instructed them in plain sewing and embroidery. Quilting could be learned in more public ways as well. Lucy Larcom remembered that in Beverly, Massachusetts, "we learned to sew patchwork at school, while we were learning the alphabet; and almost every girl, large or small, had a bed-quilt of her own begun, with an eye to future house furnishing. I was not over fond of sewing, but I thought it best to begin mine early." [11] Sarah S. Jacobs recalled of a central Massachusetts schoolhouse: "The very fathers of the town might have learned

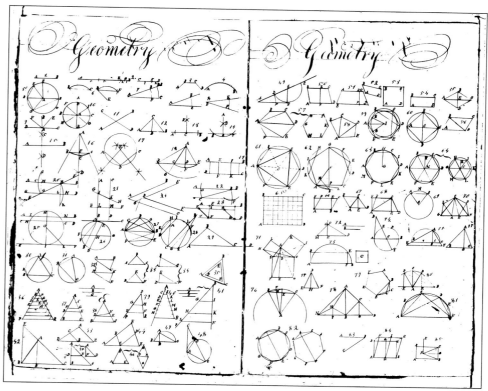

PLATE 65. *Manuscript geometry book of Elizabeth P. Jewett, Pepperell, Massachusetts, 1830. Judging by the work in this book, Elizabeth had considerably more advanced geometry skills than most quilters. She would have been able to construct the patterns for difficult pieced designs, such as the Mariner's Compass or the circular design seen on the S. S. Larkin quilt in Plate 38. [Old Sturbridge Village Research Library]*

their spelling-books, and the New England Primer,—and their girl–playmates sewed the patchwork there...."[12]

In *The Little Girl's Own Book* of 1832, Lydia Maria Child spoke directly to "little girls" about patchwork quilting. They "often have a great many small bits of cloth," she wrote, "and large remnants of time, which they don't know what to do with; and I think it is better for them to make cradle-quilts for their dolls, or their baby brothers, than to be standing around, wishing they had something to do."[13] In *The Mother's Book* of 1831 she had urged the mothers of these girls to use patchwork as a way to ensure that they learned good work habits, beginning

PLATE 66. *In the Fitch House sitting room at Old Sturbridge Village, two girls are sewing a mosaic patchwork, perhaps for a cradle quilt, while the younger children play. There is a reproduction strip-pieced doll quilt on the toy bed.*

at five or six years old. "If the corners are not fitted exactly," she advised, "or the sewing done neatly, it should be taken to pieces and fitted again; for it is by inattention to these little things that habits of carelessness are formed. On no occasion whatever should a child be excused from finishing what she has begun."[14]

Of course, not all women enjoyed quilting. A lack of aptitude for sewing could make it a miserable chore, and many were surely glad to leave it to their more talented sisters or neighbors. Lucy Larcom was one such woman. She hated needlework from childhood and many years later remembered the despair she felt at the "trial [which] confronted me in the shape of an . . . impossible patchwork quilt."[15]

Plate 67. Pieced cradle quilt of plain and printed cottons, c. 1843, from the Batchelder family of Stratham, New Hampshire. The simple piecing of this design would have made a likely project for a young girl to sew.

PLATE 68. "The Hated Task," engraving, mid-nineteenth century. [Charlotte Elizabeth (Tonna), Short Stories for Children (New York: American Tract Society, n.d.), 82.]

"To Help Them Quilt"

New England women who truly disliked quilting, or simply didn't have time to accomplish all they needed to do, at least occasionally turned to those who made quilts for pay. Cooperative household quilting predominated in New England, and there was no American version of the London quilting trade with its artisan-manufacturers. But at least as early the second decade of the eighteenth century in Boston, there seem to have been a few skilled seamstresses, like the women of the Brownell family, who found an additional use for their needle skills. In the cities they appear to have produced and sold quilts to order. In the countryside they traded their quilting skills, or finished quilts, as part of long-standing patterns of neighborhood exchange.

Elizabeth Foote of Colchester, Connecticut, noted in her diary in 1775 that she had done "two days work" for Mr. Pomroy "to help them Quilt." Rebecca Dickinson frequently made dresses for local customers in the 1780s and 1790s and may sometimes have been paid for her participation in quilting. The practice continued at least until 1840, when the seamstress L. H. Guernsey of Castleton, Vermont, noted in her diary that A. Merill owed her two dollars for "quilting 1 bed quilt," along with making window curtains and a bed valance.

The Seasons of Quilting

"In summer," Ellen H. Rollins of Wakefield, New Hampshire, observed in *New England Bygones*, quilts were "the fine needle-work of the house."[16] For most quilters today, winter is the appropriate time to head indoors and take up their needles, but early quilters' diaries revealed a very different and pronounced seasonal rhythm. The great preponderance of quilting in New England took place in the months of May through November, with much less undertaken between December and April.

One reason for this seasonal pattern was light. In a world where artificial illumination was meager, women needed sufficient daylight to see their stitching, and the long days of summer provided far more than the short days of winter with its weak sunlight. Women undertook quilting and most other sewing activities in the morning and afternoon, while preferring to do their knitting, which an experienced housewife could do almost with her eyes closed, during the hours of limited lamp- or candlelight in the evening.

Even in the light-filled months of warm weather, the diaries indicate that the number of days spent in quilting increased and declined in a regular pattern. Considering both group and individual activity together, May and October were the two busiest months of the year for quilting. Women surely welcomed the warmer weather and better light of May; probably, after winter's solitude and spring's muddy, impassable roads, they were eager to bring their friends together for an afternoon of stitching and conversation. October, the time of harvests and huskings, saw even more women working on their quilts. In between the peak times of late spring and mid-fall, quilting activity fell—although not to the low levels of mid-winter—and rose again.

Like most other activities in rural New England, the amount of time spent quilting in groups dropped significantly in late June and particularly in July, when the intensive work of haying took precedence over all other tasks. In the words of the *Maine Farmer* of 1832, these weeks constituted "the hardest part of the labor to be performed on a farm."[17] Women were often called upon to assist with raking and stacking the hay, to cook for extra hands, and to take on a greater share of chores so that men could spend more time in the fields. With so much effort devoted to haying in mid-summer, many other rhythms and routines reached their low point—even the seasonal cycle of the conception of children. It is not surprising that relatively little quilting was accomplished.

After haying season was over, quilting parties, along with other cooperative work parties like corn huskings and apple parings, started up again in August. Quilting parties peaked in September, and quilting work as a whole reached its yearly maximum in October. The late fall, especially the Thanksgiving holiday, was also "marrying time," New England's busiest season for weddings. Many late-summer and fall quilting parties were probably organized both to assist the prospective bride in making quilts for her new household and to create an

PLATE 69. *"Hay Wagon in New Hampshire," oil on canvas, by Samuel Lancaster Gerry, c. 1840. At the height of New England's haying season, as Gerry's depiction indicates, women were often called into the fields to rake and load hay. Quilting, like many other things, was postponed until haying was finished.*

opportunity for continuing courtship for her as-yet-unmarried friends. Quilting in the fall also assured that warm bedclothes would be ready for winter's long, cold nights.

In all its seasons, and in all its social settings, quilting in New England was both work and enjoyment. As Ellen Rollins recalled, "The quilting of it was hard work, but the women called this rest, and were made happy by such simple variation of labor."[18] Quilting could offer enjoyment and even solace, not only with the conviviality of company, but also with the quiet comfort of stitching in solitude. Gratefully distracted from her worries for her seafaring husband and the various family pressures that were causing her to have bad dreams, Louisa Adams Park of Acton, Massachusetts, wrote in December of 1800: "quilting all day—and happy to be so."

ENDNOTES

1. Nineteen New England diaries were examined either in the original manuscript or in published form. They are fully described in the bibliography. The quilting entries of thirteen additional diaries were also analyzed, taken from Appendix A of Lynn Bonfield, "Diaries of New England Quilters Before 1860," *Uncoverings…1988…Research Papers of the American Quilt Study Group*, vol. 9 (Mill Valley, Calif., 1989), 183-194. Only diary entries dating before 1850 are quoted here or were included in the statistical analysis.

2. Quoted in Marla R. Miller, "'My Daily Bread Depends Upon My Labor': Craftswomen, Community and the Marketplace in Rural Massachusetts, 1740-1820," unpublished Ph.D. dissertation, University of North Carolina at Chapel Hill, 1997, 149.

3. The term "quilting bee" did not come into common usage, at least in New England, until much later in the nineteenth century.

4. Francis W. Underwood, *Quabbin, the Story of a Small Town, with Outlooks on Puritan Life* (Boston: Lee and Shephard, 1893), 108-111.

5. Underwood, 108.

6. "The Patchwork Quilt," *The Lowell Offering* 5, no. 9 (September, 1845): 201-203.

7. Underwood, 116.

8. Samuel G. Goodrich, *Recollections of A Lifetime* (New York: Miller, Orton and Mulligan, 1857) vol. 1, 75.

9. T. S. Arthur, "The Quilting Party," *Godey's Lady's Book* 39, no. 4 (September, 1849): 185-6.

10. Lydia Maria Child, "The Ladies Fair," *Liberator*, January 2, 1837, 3.

11. Lucy Larcom, *A New England Girlhood* (Boston: Houghton, Mifflin and Co., 1891), 122.

12. Sarah S. Jacobs, *Nonantum and Natick* (Boston: Massachusetts Sabbath School Society, 1853), 225.

13. Child, *The Little Girl's Own Book* (Boston: Carter, Hendee and Babcock, 1832), 225.

14. Child, *The Mother's Book* (Boston: Carter, Hendee and Babcock, 1831), 61.

15. Larcom, 122.

16. Ellen H. Rollins, *New England Bygones* (Philadelphia: J. B. Lippincott & Co., 1883), 237.

17. Quoted in Jack Larkin, *The Reshaping of Everyday Life 1790-1840* (New York: HarperCollins, 1988), 19.

18. Rollins, 237.

Chapter VI

Precious Reliquaries

When This You See Remember Me

From the first time that a quilt was created out of leftover fabric scraps, women have surely been reminded of the people and events associated with those fragments of cloth. In New England, the power of patchwork quilts to evoke images of the past was already being acknowledged in 1842. An essay written for *The Lowell Offering* portrayed "The Patchwork Quilt" as an object both commonplace and precious. "Annette" (probably Harriet Farley) recalled the family members brought to mind by each scrap of patchworked fabric:

QUILTS AND QUILTING parties became picturesque symbols of an idealized past.

Yes, there is the PATCHWORK QUILT! looking to the uninterested observer like a miscellaneous collection of odd bits and ends of calico, but to me it is a precious reliquary of past treasures; a storehouse of valuables, almost destitute of worth; . . . a bound volume of hieroglyphics, each of which is a key to some painful or pleasant remembrance. . . . Gentle friends! it contains a piece of each of my childhood's calico gowns, and of my mother's and sisters. . . . [1]

Lucy Larcom recalled similar fond associations with the printed cotton fabrics from her scrapbag:

I liked assorting those little figured bits of cotton cloth, for they were scraps of gowns I had seen worn, and they reminded me of the persons who

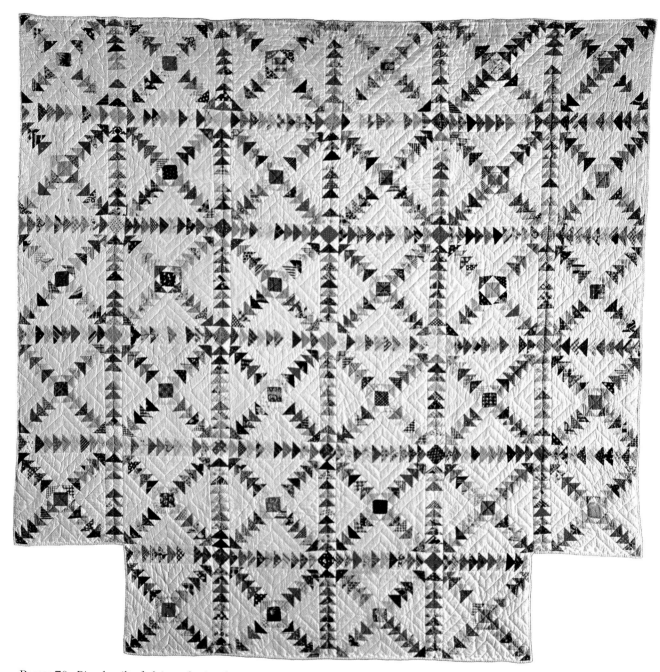

PLATE 70. *Pieced quilt of plain and printed cottons, c. 1840-1850. The scores of different calicoes used in this quilt had the power to evoke many memories—of life's milestones from childhood on, of friends and family, and of earlier generations.*

wore them. One fragment, in particular, was like a picture to me. It was a delicate pink and brown sea-moss pattern, on a white ground, a piece of a dress belonging to my married sister, who was to me bride and angel in one. I always saw her face before me when I unfolded this scrap....[2]

The "friendship" quilts that came into fashion in the 1840s were a reminder of the powerful emotions that could become invested in "scraps of calico." In an era devoted to the cultivation of sentiment, they emerged out of the earlier nineteenth-century New England practice of keeping bound albums on whose pages women gathered expressions of love and concern, quotations, verses, and the signatures of friends and relatives.

Like today's souvenir albums and yearbooks, friendship quilts were documents of remembrance; individual patchwork blocks were signed by friends and relatives of the quilt's recipient. More often than not, friendship quilts commemorated partings. In the 1840s, as in previous decades, these were due in approximately equal measure to two great streams of migration: one westward, from crowded rural New England to the new farmlands of Michigan, Illinois, and Iowa; and the other from the countryside to the cities and manufacturing towns. In their hopes of finding new prosperity, many New England families pulled themselves away from their native communities. Western migration involved greater distances, but most moves meant long separations and infrequent visits, if any. Migration was hardest on women, who followed in the wake of their husbands' ambitions and often felt wrenched away from everyone and everything they had known. Friendship quilts provided a tangible link to the friends and family left behind—who might never be seen again.

Friendship quilts were also made for such noteworthy events as marriages and births. The recipient of the friendship quilt in Plate 71 is not known, but it was obviously created for her in great affection. It is made of both plain and printed cottons in the Irish chain pattern, and its design and fabrics have clearly been chosen with considerable care. In the diamond-shaped blocks of plain white cotton around the border, it is signed by over fifty members of the Torrey, Curtis, Tirrell, and Dyer families, who lived in close proximity to each other in

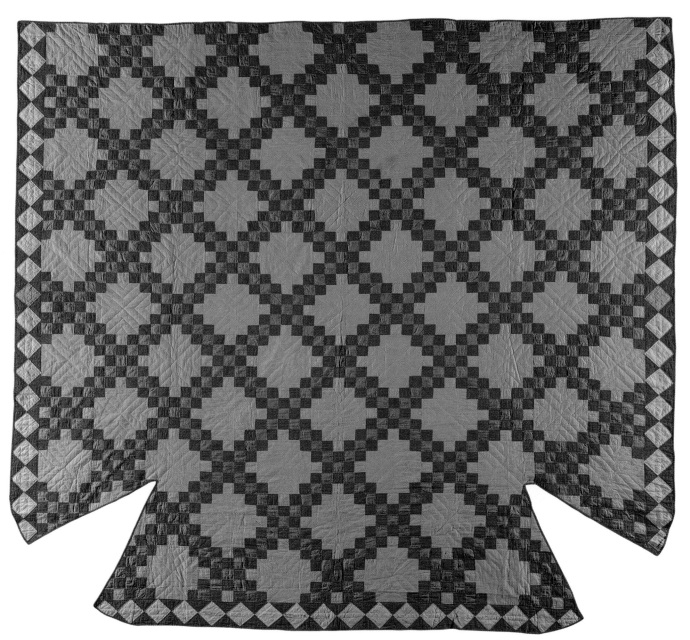

PLATE 71. *Pieced friendship quilt of plain and printed cottons, c. 1845-1850. The white diamonds around the quilt's border have been signed, and sometimes inscribed, by over fifty individuals from South Weymouth, Massachusetts, and neighboring communities.*

PLATE 72. *(Detail) Pieced friendship quilt of plain cottons, c. 1845-1850. This small diamond patch is signed "Hannah B. Stowell" and inscribed "Friendship," both in ink.*

South Weymouth, Massachusetts. A few assorted friends from neighboring communities also signed the quilt. Perhaps it was made as a wedding gift, for it has not traveled far from where it was created; also, a number of the young women who signed it were married within five years of its completion, suggesting that the recipient was also a member of their age group.

The Romance of the Patchwork Quilt

By the middle of the nineteenth century, New England's patchwork quilts were coming to embody a paradox. The revolutions in commerce and industry had democratized quiltmaking by dramatically lowering the cost of fabric so that poor and middling families could afford printed calicoes and have abundant scraps; but they also worked to undermine the rural lifeways in which patchwork quilts and quilting parties had become rooted. As economic opportunity drew more and more people away from rural communities and into crowded, busy cities and manufacturing towns, quilts and quilting parties became symbols of the loss of a "simpler" way of life.

Despite its relatively recent origins, after a few decades the pieced calico quilt began to seem an old tradition of the countryside, an antique handicraft. Thus, as some makers of fashion scoffed at patchwork quilts, other writers began to romanticize them. "Annette" dramatized the pieced quilt as an artifact of the past in *The Lowell Offering* while writing from the heart of the factory system, in America's showplace industrial city. In 1849 *Godey's Lady's Book* combined its up-to-date fashion plates with a nostalgic description of the traditional "Quilting Party." The author, T. S. Arthur, a best-selling novelist of domestic life in the mid-nineteenth century, put his story well in the past, assuming (inaccurately, as we know) that young American women no longer knew anything of patchwork, quilting, or cooperative work. [3] In 1856 Stephen Foster's song, "The Quilting Party" recounted "seeing Nellie home" as an early, sentimental memory of courtship in the countryside:

> In the sky the bright stars glittered,
> On the bank the pale moon shone;
> And t'was from Aunt Dinah's quilting party
> I was seeing Nellie home
> I was seeing Nellie home
> I was seeing Nellie home
> And t'was from Aunt Dinah's quilting party
> I was seeing Nellie home.
>
> On my arm a soft hand rested,
> Rested light as foam;
>
> On my lips a whisper trembled,
> Trembled till it dared to come;
>
> On my life new hopes were dawning,
> And those hopes have liv'd and grown. [4]

In Catharine Maria Sedgwick's story of 1846, "The Patch-Work Quilt" became a metaphor for New England's early history. Pondering a pieced quilt made of the clothing scraps from past generations, the story's protagonist sees its fabrics, from "Queen Anne's broadcloths" to later cotton prints, as images of the succeeding generations in a New England town since its first settlement by Europeans. It provides a "patchwork history" of the community's earlier years, but there have been far more dramatic changes since: the woods have been cleared to feed industrial furnaces, the railway holds sway on the old "bridle path," science has "changed the aspect of the world," and "families have multiplied and sent forth members to join the grand procession towards Oregon.... All these changes, and the patch-work-quilt remains in its first gloss!" [5]

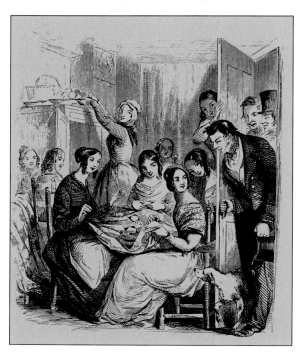

PLATE 73. *"The Quilting Party," engraving,* Godey's Lady's Book *[Vol. 39 No. 9 (September 1849)]*

In these stories and songs patchwork quilts and quilting parties are part of a vanishing world. They were part of a larger lament about social change, one that was probably heard earlier in New England than anywhere else in the United States, as the region swiftly became the most urbanized and industrialized part of the United States.

Of course, the art of piecing quilts and the practice of quilting in social groups were never completely lost in New England—or elsewhere in America. Thousands of surviving pieced-block quilts, along with oral histories, photographs, and memoirs all document the persistence of quilting as a particularly rural tradition throughout the nineteenth and early twentieth centuries. But city-dwelling Americans became more and more distant from this world, and for many of them quilting evoked a "lost" rural America far in the past. Such nostalgia grew even stronger as the nation prepared for the Centennial Celebration of 1876. In displays, demonstrations, and nostalgic writing, romantic regional historians found in quilts and quilting parties picturesque symbols of an idealized past in which everyone was hard-working, cooperative, frugal, and productive.

In recent years, that sentimental approach to quilts has given way to more careful scholarship that is trying to develop a new understanding of America's quilts and quiltmakers of the eighteenth, nineteenth, and early twentieth centuries. We still cherish quilts for their beauty and their ability to link us to the American past, but our love for them can be grounded in a deeper comprehension of what these quilts meant to their makers and to their times—and what they mean to us.

ENDNOTES

1. "The Patchwork Quilt," *The Lowell Offering,* 5, no. 9 (September, 1845): 201-203.
2. Lucy Larcom, *A New England Girlhood* (Boston: Houghton, Mifflin and Company, 1891), 122-123.
3. T. S. Arthur, "The Quilting Party," *Godey's Lady's Book.* 39, no. 4 (September, 1849): 185-6.
4. Quoted in Averil Colby, *Quilting* (New York: Charles Scribner's Sons, 1971), 143; see also John Christopher, *The Biggest Little Songbook* (McAfee Music Corporation, 1973), 14.
5. Catharine Maria Sedgwick, "The Patch-Work Quilt," *The Columbian Lady's and Gentleman's Magazine* 5 (March 1846). Reprinted in Cuesta Ray Benberry and Carol Pinney Crabb, *A Patchwork of Pieces: An Anthology of Early Quilt Stories, 1845-1940* (Paducah, Ky.: American Quilter's Society, 1993), 32-33.

Bibliography

PRINTED PRIMARY SOURCES

"Annette" (Harriet Farley). "The Patchwork Quilt." *The Lowell Offering*, 5, no. 9 (September, 1845): 201-203

Arthur, T. S. "The Quilting Party." *Godey's Lady's Book* 39, no. 4 (September, 1849): 185-6.

Barber, John Warner. *Massachusetts Historical Collections.* Worcester, Mass.: Dorr and Howland, 1840.

Bemiss, Elijah. *The Dyer's Companion.* New London, Conn.: Cady and Eells, 1806.

Benberry, Cuesta Ray and Carol Pinney Crabb. *A Patchwork of Pieces: An Anthology of Early Quilt Stories, 1845-1940.* Paducah, Ky.: American Quilter's Society, 1993.

Bronson, J. and R. *The Domestic Manufacturer's Assistant, and Family Directory in the Arts of Weaving and Dyeing.* Utica, N.Y.: William Williams, 1817.

Child, Lydia Maria. *The American Frugal Housewife.* Boston: Carter, Hendee and Babcock, 1833.

———. "The Ladies' Fair." *The Liberator,* January 2, 1837.

———. *The Little Girl's Own Book.* Boston: Carter, Hendee and Babcock, 1832.

———. *The Mother's Book.* Boston: Carter, Hendee and Babcock, 1831.

Cook, Clarence, ed. *A Girl's Life Eighty Years Ago: Selections from the Letters of Eliza Southgate Bowne.* New York: Charles Scribner's Sons, 1887.

Davis, George. *A Historical Sketch of Sturbridge and Southbridge.* West Brookfield, Mass.: Power Press of O. S. Cooke and Co., 1856.

Domestic Economy: Being a Treatise on the Arts of Dyeing and Cleaning of Clothing, Beds, Carpets, &c. Rochester, N.Y.: William Alling, 1841.

Dow, George Francis, ed. *The Holyoke Diaries,* 1709-1856. Salem, Mass.: The Essex Institute, 1911.

Ellis, Asa Jr. *The Country Dyer's Assistant.* Brookfield, Mass.: E. Merriam and Co., 1798.

Goodrich, Samuel G. *Recollections of A Lifetime.* Vol. 1. New York: Miller, Orton, and Mulligan, 1857.

(Hartford) *Connecticut Courant* 1795-1798

Holbrook, Jay Mack, comp. *Vital Records for the Town of Ware, Massachusetts, 1735-1893.* Oxford, Mass.: Jay Mack Holbrook, 1983. Microfiche.

Jacobs, Sarah S. *Nonantum and Natick.* Boston: Massachusetts Sabbath School Society, 1853.

Larcom, Lucy. *A New England Girlhood.* Boston: Houghton Mifflin Co., 1891.

Leslie, Eliza. *American Girl's Book, or, Occupation for play hours.* Boston: Monroe and Francis, 1831.

———. *The House Book: or, A Manual of Domestic Economy.* Philadelphia: Carey and Hart, 1843.

Massachusetts Charitable Mechanic Association … *The Massachusetts Charitable Mechanic Association … Third Exhibition for the Encouragement of Manufactures and the Mechanic Arts …* Boston, 1841.

Montgomery, James. *A Practical Detail of the Cotton Manufacture of the United States of America.* Glasgow: John Niven, Jr., 1840.

Pullan, Mrs. *The Lady's Manual of Fancy-Work.* New York: Dick and Fitzgerald, 1858.

Rollins, Ellen H. *New England Bygones.* Philadelphia: J. B. Lippincott and Co., 1883.

Underwood, Francis H. *Quabbin, The Story of a Small Town with Outlooks Upon Puritan Life.* Boston: Lee and Shepard, 1893.

(Worcester) *Massachusetts Spy* 1834-1840.

The Workwoman's Guide. London: Simpkin, Marshall, and Co., 1838.

MANUSCRIPT PRIMARY SOURCES

Butler, John. Account Book. Ashford, Conn., 1794-1828. Old Sturbridge Village Research Library.

Devotion, Jonathan and Co. Account Book. Windham, Conn., 1795-1800. Old Sturbridge Village Research Library.

Probate Inventories for Sturbridge, Massachusetts, 1735-1850. Transcriptions by Holly V. Izard from Worcester County, Massachusetts, Probate Records. Microfilm at Old Sturbridge Village Research Library.

Probate Records for the Anderson family of Ware, Hampshire County, Massachusetts, Probate Records, boxes 4, 275, 319. Hampshire County Hall of Records, Northampton, Mass.

Schedules of the Federal Population Census for Massachusetts, 1820-1830-1840-1850. Microfilm at Old Sturbridge Village Research Library.

Storrs, Daniel. Day Book. Mansfield, Conn., 1788. Old Sturbridge Village Research Library.

PUBLISHED QUILTING DIARIES

Ayer, Sarah Connell (Andover and Newburyport, Mass.; Concord and Bow, N.H.; Portland and Eastport, Maine, 1805-1835). *Diary of Sarah Connell Ayer.* Portland, Maine: Lefavor-Tower Co., 1910.

Ballard, Martha Moore (Hallowell, Maine, 1785-1812). In Charles Elventon Nash, *The History of Augusta,* 235-464. Augusta, Maine: Charles E. Nash and Son, 1904.

Brown, Sally and Pamela. Bryant, Blanche Brown and Gertrude Elaine Baker, eds. *The Diaries of Sally and Pamela Brown, 1832-1838, and Hyde Leslie, 1887, Plymouth Notch, Vermont.* Springfield, Vt.: William L. Bryant Foundation, 1970.

Fuller, Elizabeth (Princeton, Mass., 1790-1792). In Frances Everett Blake, *History of The Town of Princeton,* 303-

322. Princeton, Mass.: Published by the Town, 1915.

Phelps, Elizabeth Porter. (Hadley, Mass., 1763-1805).

Andrews, Thomas Eliot, ed. "The Diary of Elizabeth (Porter) Phelps." Parts 1-19 *The New England Historical and Genealogical Register* 118 (January-October, 1964): 1-30, 108-139, 219-235, 297-308; 119 (January-October, 1965): 43-59, 127-140, 203-223, 289-307; 120 (January-October, 1966): 57-62, 123-135, 203-214, 293-304; 121 (January-April, October, 1967): 57-69, 95-100, 296-303; 122 (January-October, 1968): 62-70, 115-123, 220-227, 302-309.

Shepard, David.

Rose, Alexander G. III, ed. *The Chester and Westfield, Mass., Diaries (1795-1798) of David Shepard, Jr.* Baltimore: 1975.

Winslow, Anna Green.

Earle, Alice Morse., ed. *Diary of Anna Green Winslow, a Boston School Girl of 1771.* Boston and New York: Houghton Mifflin Co., 1894.

MANUSCRIPT QUILTING DIARIES

Bascom, Ruth Henshaw. Leicester, Mass., 1789-1800 (years examined). American Antiquarian Society, Worcester, Mass.

Bradley, Harriet P. Watertown, Conn., 1819-1820. Old Sturbridge Village Research Library.

Bryant, Sarah Snell. Cummington, Mass., 1794. Bryant Homestead, Trustees of Reservations, Cummington, Mass.

————. Cummington, Mass., 1796-1835. Houghton Library, Harvard University, Cambridge.

Dickinson, Rebecca. Hatfield, Mass., 1787-1802. (Transcribed and edited by Marla Miller). Flynt Library, Pocumtuck Valley Memorial Association, Deerfield, Mass.

Foote, Abigail. Colchester, Conn., 1775-1776. Connecticut Historical Society, Hartford.

Foote, Elizabeth. Colchester, Conn., 1775. Connecticut Historical Society, Hartford.

Guernsey, L. H. Castleton, Vt., 1834-1845. Old Sturbridge Village Research Library.

Leonard, Jerusha. Sunderland, Mass., 1791-1792. Flynt Library, Pocumtuck Valley Memorial Association, Deerfield, Mass.

Park, Louisa Adams. Acton, Mass., 1800-1801. American Antiquarian Society, Worcester, Mass.

Roberts, Candace. Bristol, Conn., 1801-1806. Public Library, Bristol, Conn.

Smith, Julia Evelina. Glastonbury, Conn., 1827. Connecticut Historical Society, Hartford.

White, Mary Avery. Boylston, Mass., 1836-1849. Old Sturbridge Village Research Library.

SECONDARY SOURCES

Berenson, Katherine. *Quilts of Provence, the Art and Craft of French Quiltmaking.* New York: Henry Holt and Company, 1996.

Bonfield, Lynn A. "Diaries of New England Quilters Before 1860." In *Uncoverings...1988...Research Papers of the American Quilt Study Group,* vol. 9, 171-197. San Francisco: American Quilt Study Group, 1989.

————. "The Production of Cloth, Clothing and Quilts in 19th-Century New England Homes." In *Uncoverings...1981...Research Papers of the American Quilt Study Group,* vol. 2, 77-96. Mill Valley, Calif.: American Quilt Study Group, 1982.

Brackman, Barbara. "A Chronological Index to Pieced Quilt Patterns, 1775-1825." In *Uncoverings...1983...Research Papers of the American Quilt Study Group,* vol. 4, 99-127. Mill Valley, Calif.: American Quilt Study Group, 1984.

————. *Clues in the Calico: A Guide to Identifying and Dating Antique Quilts.* McLean, Va.: EPM Publications, Inc., 1989.

————. "Cut-out Chintz Applique: A Historical Perspective." *Quilter's Newsletter Magazine* 27, no. 9 (Nov. 1996): 30-34.

————. "Fairs and Expositions: Their Influence on American Quilts." In *Bits and Pieces: Textile Traditions,* edited by Jeanette Lasansky, 91-99. Lewisburg, Pa.: Oral Traditions Project, 1991.

————. "Signature Quilts: Nineteenth-Century Trends." In *Uncoverings...1989...Research Papers of the American Quilt Study Group,* vol. 10, 25-37. San Francisco: American Quilt Study Group, 1990.

————. "What's in a Name? Quilt Patterns from 1830 to the Present." In *Pieced By Mother,* edited by Jeanette Lasansky, 107-114. Lewisburg, Pa.: Oral Traditions Project, 1988.

Bullard, Lacy Folmar and Betty Jo Shiell. *Chintz Quilts: Unfading Glory.* Tallahassee, Fla.: Serendipity Publishers, 1983.

Bushman, Richard L. *The Refinement of America, Persons, Houses, Cities.* New York: Vintage Books, 1993.

Callahan, Colleen. "A Quilt and Its Pieces." *Metropolitan Museum Journal* 19-20 (1986): 97-141.

Chase, Arthur. *History of Ware, Massachusetts.* Cambridge, Mass.: The University Press, 1911.

Church, Diana. "The Baylis Stenciled Quilt." In *Uncoverings...1983 ...Research Papers of the American Quilt Study Group,* vol. 4, 75-86. Mill Valley, Calif.: American Quilt Study Group, 1984.

Clark, Ricky. "Fragile Families: Quilts as Kinship Bonds." In *The Quilt Digest,* vol. 5, 4-19. San Francisco: The Quilt Digest Press, 1987.

Cleveland, Richard L. and Donna Bister. *Plain and Fancy: Vermont's People and Their Quilts as a Reflection of America.* Gualala, Calif.: The Quilt Digest Press, 1991.

Cochran, Rachel, et al. *New Jersey Quilts 1777-1950: Contributions to an American Tradition.* Paducah, Ky.: American Quilter's Society, 1992.

Colby, Averil. *Quilting.* New York: Charles Scribner's Sons, 1971.

Cummins, Hazel E. "Calamanco." *The Magazine Antiques* 39, no. 4 (April 1941): 182-184.

Dow, George Francis. *The Arts & Crafts in New England 1704-1775.* Topsfield, Mass.: The Wayside Press, 1927.

Fitzrandolph, Mavis. *Traditional Quilting, Its Story and Its Practice.* Boston: Boston Book and Art Shop, 1954.

Fox, Sandi. *For Purpose and Pleasure, Quilting Together in Nineteenth-*

Century America. Nashville: Rutledge Hill Press, 1995.

Garoutte, Sally. "Cloth in North America in the 17th and 18th Centuries: Sources and Distribution." In *Book of Papers, National Textile Conference... 1977*, 132-136. Research Triangle Park, N.C.: American Textile Chemists and Colorists, 1977.

———. "Early Colonial Quilts in a Bedding Context." In *Uncoverings...1980...Research Papers of the American Quilt Study Group*, vol. 1, 18-25. Mill Valley, Calif.: American Quilt Study Group, 1981.

———. "Marseilles Quilts and their Woven Offspring." In *Uncoverings...1982...Research Papers of the American Quilt Study Group*, vol. 3, 115-134. Mill Valley, Calif.: American Quilt Study Group, 1983.

Gunn, Virginia. "Template Quilt Construction and its Offshoots." In *Pieced By Mother*, edited by Jeanette Lasansky, 69-75. Lewisburg, Pa.: Oral Traditions Project, 1988.

Hake, Elizabeth. *English Quilting Old & New*. New York: Charles Scribner's Sons, 1937.

Halpern, Nancy. "Special Exhibit: The Wool Quilts of New England." Exhibit notes, Vermont Quilt Festival, 1984.

Hefford, Wendy. *The Victoria and Albert Museum's Textile Collection*. Vol. 1, *Design for Printed Textiles in England from 1750 to 1850*. London: Victoria & Albert Enterprises, 1992.

Hersh, Tandy. "18th Century Quilted Silk Petticoats Worn in America." In *Uncoverings...1984...Research Papers of the American Quilt Study Group*, vol. 5, 83-98. Mill Valley, Calif.: American Quilt Study Group, 1985.

———. "Quilted Petticoats." In *Pieced By Mother*, edited by Jeannette Lasansky, 5-11. Lewisburg, Pa.: Oral Traditions Project, 1988.

———. "Some Aspects of an 1809 Quilt." In *Uncoverings...1982... Research Papers of the American Quilt Study Group*, vol. 3, 3-12. Mill Valley, Calif.: American Quilt Study Group, 1983.

Jeremy, David J. *Transatlantic Industrial Revolution: The Diffusion of Textile Technologies Between Britain and America, 1790-1830s*. Cambridge, Mass.: The MIT Press, for the Merrimack Valley Textile Museum, 1981.

Larkin, Jack. *The Reshaping of Everyday Life, 1790-1840*. New York: Harper Collins, 1988.

Lasansky, Jeanette. "T-Shaped Quilts: A New England Phenomenon." *The Magazine Antiques* 152, no. 6 (December, 1997): 842-845.

Miall, Agnes M. *Patchwork Old and New*. London: The Woman's Magazine Office, 1937.

Miller, Marla. "'My Daily Bread Depends Upon My Labor': Craftswomen, Community and the Marketplace in Rural Massachusetts, 1740-1820." Ph.D. diss., University of North Carolina at Chapel Hill, 1997.

Montgomery, Florence. *Printed Textiles, English and American Cottons and Linens 1700-1850*. New York: The Viking Press, 1970.

———. *Textiles in America, 1650-1870*. New York: W. W. Norton and Company, 1984.

Nicoll, Jessica F. *Quilted for Friends: Delaware Valley Signature Quilts, 1840-1855*. Winterthur, Del.: H. F. DuPont Winterthur Museum, 1986.

———. "Rainbow Shapes & Faint Traceries." *Old Sturbridge Visitor* 30, no. 4 (Winter, 1990): 4-6.

Nylander, Jane. *Our Own Snug Fireside: Images of the New England Home 1760-1860*. New York: Alfred. A. Knopf, 1993.

Oliver, Celia Y. *Enduring Grace, Quilts from the Shelburne Museum Collection*. Lafayette, Calif.: C & T Publishing, 1997.

Osler, Dorothy. *Traditional British Quilts*. London: B. T. Batsford, Ltd., 1987.

Peck, Amelia. *American Quilts and Coverlets in The Metropolitan Museum of Art*. New York: Metropolitan Museum of Art, 1990.

Rae, Janet. *The Quilts of the British Isles*. New York: E. P. Dutton, 1987.

———, et al. *Quilt Treasures of Great Britain, The Heritage Search of the Quilters' Guild*. Nashville: Rutledge Hill Press, 1995.

Ring, Betty. *Girlhood Embroidery, American Samplers & Pictorial Needlework, 1650-1850*. Vol. 1. New York: Alfred. A. Knopf, 1993.

Riznik, Barnes. "New England Wool-Carding and Finishing Mills, 1790-1840." Research report, Old Sturbridge Village, 1964.

Smith, Wilene. "Quilt Blocks—Or Quilt Patterns?" In *Quiltmaking in America: Beyond the Myths*, edited by Laurel Horton, 30-39. Nashville: Rutledge Hill Press, 1994.

Stachiw, Myron O. "The Color of Change: A Nineteenth-Century Massachusetts House." In *Paint in America: The Colors of Historic Buildings*, edited by Roger W. Moss, 128-137. Washington, D.C.: National Trust for Historic Preservation, 1994.

Storey, Joyce B. "Turkey Red Prints: A Happy Blend of Art and Technology." *Surface Design Journal* 20, no. 4 (Summer 1996): 7-8, 34-35, 38.

Tuckhorn, Nancy Gibson. "The Assimilation of German Folk Designs on Maryland Quilts." *The Magazine Antiques* 149, no. 2 (February, 1996): 304-313.

Ulrich, Laurel Thatcher. *A Midwife's Tale: The Life of Martha Ballard, Based on Her Diary, 1785-1812*. New York: Alfred A. Knopf, 1990.

Victoria and Albert Museum. *Notes on Quilting*. London: His Majesty's Stationery Office, 1949.

Warren, Elizabeth V. and Sharon L. Eisenstat. *Glorious American Quilts: The Quilt Collection of The Museum of American Folk Art*. New York: Penguin Studio, 1996.

Index